Is It Too Late To Get My Money Back?

Christine Pechacek

The events written are an account of our lives as husband and wife. Every effort has been made to be as accurate as possible with regard to facts and events, times and places. Where an * appears, names have been changed.

Scripture quotations are taken from The Living Bible. Copyright© 1971 by Tyndale House Publishers, Wheaton, Illinois 60187.

IS IT TOO LATE TO GET MY MONEY BACK?
Copyright © 2013 Christine Pechacek

All rights reserved.
ISBN: 0988878119
ISBN 13: 9780988878112
Library of Congress Control Number: 2013917612
OnPoint Publishing LLC, Harrison, MI

ACKNOWLEDGMENTS

Distance and time create a safe bridge over which to walk and visit our past. As a visitor, it is tempting to want to rewrite the painful portions. You love that person who once was you and cringe at the hurt you know is coming as you inch closer to the memories. It is natural to want to use the eraser, the whiteout, the backspace key or delete button in order to rewrite your history. I wanted that Christine to be bolder, smarter, and at times, nastier. But I did not rewrite, erase or delete. It may seem as the pages unfold, that I was alone and helpless; a victim. That was never the case. Every step I have taken, and continue to walk is orchestrated and watched over. And my road is crowded with lush places that have made me who I am.

Carrie, Twila and Cassie, three women who, over our now forty-five years of friendship, continue to show me what love and loyalty are all about. We laugh together, we cry together and we have even plotted, planned, but never carried out, some ingenious revenge together. You have kept me grounded and sane over the years, holding on to me when life threatened to become untethered and I just wanted to float away. I love each one of you.

Linda, our once a week lunches nourish me in a way food never can. You pray for me and over me, lifting my spirit beyond what my eyes see or my hands touch. And I once again know what is real. You must never give up being the magnificent RN you are.

Esther, you are, and have been, my friend 'for such a time as this.' You were an anchor when life threatened to push me out to sea, alone and afraid. You taught me the beauty of truth and the beast of faithfulness. Joyce, you pointed the way, put the key in my hand, and waited patiently as I walked my own way. Peggy, your honest and raw love of Jesus Christ made me starve for the same. You taught me by your life the beauty and absolute joy in prayer and in trusting God to be who He says He is.

Julie and Samuel, you are my two greatest accomplishments. You give back to me one thousand-fold every day of your lives. What magnificent human beings you are. If only for you, it was worth every day. I would do it all again in a heartbeat just to know you.

My beautiful daughter-in-law, Stacy, you were so right about the cover. Thank you. Sarah, thank you for being that second set of eyes when I most needed it. You are more than a friend.

Daniel, we are approaching one half century of being together, sharing misery and pain, too much of which we ourselves caused, laughter and joy, and dodging bullets; the ones we fired at each other and the ones fired upon us by friend and foe alike. It never mattered, not really. Time and time again we have circled our wagons, held tight and fought our way back to where we belong— together. We have each other.

Helen Wener MacDonald

1919 – 2010

My Aunt Helen.

AUTHOR'S NOTE

The following contain chapters I did not want to write. These are places I did not want to ever go again. This is the pain I kept at bay for far too long. But if they are not written, the wounds remain hidden to continue their deadly work unseen, until, having devoured the soul, quietly steal away. These are the emotions that Dan and I have weathered, been thrust through, survived, and became stronger. These are the places we hate re-visiting. The days turned to weeks as I conjured up excuse after excuse for not putting pen to paper.

For a complete story to be understood, the telling must be true, the emotions real, and unmasked. The pages tell who we were then and who we have become. While traveling the long shadowy roads, my grief took me places I never want to go again, but do not curse God for having taken me. My sincere prayer is that out of the pit, and through the prisons, my readers will stay with me to experience the palace.

INTRODUCTION

When my oldest granddaughter, Madison, was two-years-old, she was joined by a brother, Noah. As Noah learned to sit up, Julie, my daughter, would bathe them together. As sometimes happens when relaxation begins, Noah would emit small surprises into the bath water. Normally Madison was bathed and out of harm's way by then. Occasionally however, if she lingered too long or Julie was not quick enough. . . plop, to the surface.

On one such occasion, to Madison's horror and Julie's perverse sense of humor. . . plop, plop, plop, appeared on the water's surface in rapid succession.

Madison was up from the bath water like a rocket propelled at warp speed.

"Get me out of here!" she screamed.

Julie, already leaning on the side of the tub, grabbed Madison and plucked her quickly from the menacing projectiles. Noah, oblivious to his faux-pas and the ensuing panic, sat calmly watching the flurry taking place around him.

As I think back on the early years of my married life, my granddaughter's words echo with truth for my own experiences.

APRIL, 1970

The pain was unbearable. Something was wrong, more wrong that I could ever imagine wrong could be.

I lay flat on my back on a narrow hospital bed in the emergency room. Someone told me I would be going into surgery soon. My chest was on fire with pain that never let up. The monster inside of me pounded away like a thousand searing sledge hammers. This pain did not come in waves, leaving me seconds to gasp a full breath. It was unrelenting in its ferocity.

Exhausted from now eight hours of doing battle with my own body, I wanted to fade into an abyss of sleep. If I could just close my eyes. . . but the savage pain tore through me, reminding me that I had lost control of my body hours ago.

Someone sat down on a small stool situated on the floor nearest my head. I looked into a stranger's eyes.

"I'm your anesthesiologist. I'll be helping you to sleep for surgery," he said, "and I'll be with you throughout." His voice was quiet, unhurried.

The words made little sense to me. I groaned, pushing my torso up with my elbows, trying to get away from the weight of pain that continued to drive and slice its way up and into my shoulders. It was useless. Gurgling, choking sounds came from my throat. My body shook uncontrollably. I was cold but also terrified. I did not know if the spasms racking my frame were from the cold or the growing terror at what now seemed my hopeless situation.

The person sitting next to my bed on wheels put a warm hand on my cheek. His touch was soft but barely registered in my head. The pain screamed, drowning out the incoming touch.

"Why?" The word came out in a strangled sound. Warm tears slid down the sides of my icy temples. My arms seemed paralyzed, unable to raise my hand to wipe the tears away. Every nerve in my body was focused on the pain. "Why would God do this?" I groaned.

In answer, or because he had no answer, the man touched my face again.

Two months earlier my Doctor had confirmed what we had anticipated. I was pregnant. Danny and I had been trying to get pregnant for four years with no success. Endless tests had shown no obvious problems and no reason why I could not conceive. Finally, now, it was true. Our five-year-old daughter, Julie, would have a baby brother or sister and Michael would be an uncle once more. I was both happy and relieved. The months turned into years had convinced me of my failure, both as a wife and as a woman. Frustration often turned to anger. What was wrong with me? Why did my body refuse to do what it was supposed to do? The questions had turned to self-recrimination.

Danny had never said he was unhappy or disappointed, but I sensed something was not right. I was convinced this pregnancy would make whatever it was all good again. Friends congratulated us. Our families were thrilled. But nothing could compare with my own feelings of exaltation.

Two months into the pregnancy, a short eight weeks, it happened. I was sound asleep in a warm bed. It was 2 a.m. Suddenly an explosion went off in my stomach. I sat up and grabbed my belly.

"Danny," I said as I shook his shoulder to wake him up from his sound sleep.

"What?" Half awake, he leaned towards me.

"Something's wrong," I said. "Something happened."

"What?" He was waking up fast. "What do you mean?"

"I don't know. My stomach," I doubled over. "It hurts. I don't know." Panic was beginning to make its way into my voice.

"Are you bleeding?" he asked.

"I don't know," my voice was weak, nausea rolling in my stomach and rising up my throat.

"You better check," he said.

I rolled over to put my feet on the floor and felt it; a hot, searing stab. The quick, sharp pain halted my attempt to get out of bed.

"What's wrong?" Danny asked.

"It hurts to move." I stopped and waited.

"Well, okay, go slow," he told me. "Here, let me help you." He got out of bed, came around to me and took my hand.

Slowly inching my way first to sit up and then to slide out of bed, a black wave rolled over me. "I'm going to faint," I whispered. And then everything went black.

Seconds later, I opened my eyes to my husband's face close to mine.

"I'm calling the doctor," he said. After explaining what was happening, I heard Danny say into the phone, "Okay. We'll try that."

"What did he say?" I asked.

"He said you're probably constipated," Danny did not sound convinced. "He said to give you an enema."

I shook my head, not quite comprehending the logic. But anything that helped me stay away from any idea that might suggest trouble with the pregnancy was one I embraced.

For the next several hours we held onto the thought and hope that this pain was a simple fix with a logical explanation.

My husband of just six years prepared to administer an enema on my barely conscious form. I was unable to remain conscious if I even attempted to sit up. Danny held me up, his arms locked around me to lead me to the bathroom. I fainted. Seconds later, he tried again. Blackness again. Finally, he lifted me up and carried me to the bathroom and lay me on the floor. The cold tiles felt good. Pressure in my chest pulsed louder. I wanted to stretch, put my shoulders back to make room for whatever was throbbing and building to greater heights in my chest. Each attempt met with fresh pain and darkness.

Danny sat me up on the toilet seat, put my shoulders back and looked at me. Oblivion hit and I collapsed into his arms. After administering the enema, he carried me back to our bedroom. His attempts to lay me on the bed brought indescribable pain that, at first made me cry out, and then, the abyss. Finally, he carefully sat me on the floor, my back resting against the bed. My head down, my chin resting on my chest, I alternated between cries and whimpers. Blacking out became my only respite from the monster inside me.

The awful reality of what was happening was still to come for both of us.

At 8 a.m., after another call to the doctor, Danny, who insisted that my pain was getting worse, not better, was instructed to bring me into the office. In retrospect, it seems ludicrous that we remained blatantly naïve in such a life-threatening situation. But, as had been all our young and now adult lives, we were on our own with no older, wiser heads to guide us.

Unable to stay conscious, which rendered walking on my own out of the question, my husband carried me into the doctor's office. Within minutes, we were ordered to the nearest emergency room.

I heard the quiet voice again, "They're taking you into surgery very soon," he whispered. "The surgeon will be here shortly."

I forced my eyes open and looked in the direction of the voice. I stared at him, my eyes losing focus as I thrust my head from side to side. My breaths came in gasps, shortened each time by the jack-hammer thrusts in my chest and shoulders. I panted, every breath coming forth in a grunting growl. Blacking out would be a mercy if only for a brief moment. But even that would not come. Instead, new fists of pain came to snatch me, angrily pulling me back from the merciful black of unconsciousness.

Two nurses stood over me as one explained she would be start-ing an IV in my arm. One gently held my arm as the other began probing for a vein. Minutes later and numerous attempts to find a vein that had not already collapsed, the IV needle was in, bringing fluids into my body.

Left alone, I rolled from side to side, desperate for one brief moment without the agony clawing at my body. Instead, it increased and seemed to rise up to new heights. I dug into the sheets with my heels, trying to push up and away from the knife-like stabs that now came faster and more violently. I sobbed in full-blown panic.

And then, his face. My husband leaned over me, his face just inches from mine. He took my hand in both of his and held it to his chest and then to his face, now wet with tears. He did not speak. His eyes followed mine as I thrashed my head back and forth. I slowed my movements and stared into his face.

Two things are seared into my memory of that day. The first is the look on my young husband's face. His handsome features were strained and haggard; his eyes, red, clouded with tears. His lips parted slightly, as he sucked in a sob. There was genuine fear on his face that settled in his beautiful brown eyes. There was desperation, in the strong shoulders and chest that leaned over and close to me. Desperation at how helpless he was to stop this horror; and fear, as he came to the realization that his wife might just die here, today, in a hospital emergency room.

We did not speak. In those brief, insane, agonizing moments, something happened that seared a bond between us. Not spoken, but forged.

The second occurred moments later.

A nurse appeared and quietly told Danny it was time for my surgery. The pain was now beyond telling. What had been fear now exploded into abject terror.

As I was being slowly wheeled away from my husband, I gasped, "It hurts so bad. I can't stand it," I groaned the words. "Can I scream? Is it all right to scream?" I looked at my husband's eyes for reassurance.

His tears came out in a rush, "Yes," he said between his own sobs. "Yes, you can scream."

And so I did. Long, loud, continuous screams.

The swinging doors shut and I was in a hallway, my bed up against a wall. I was alone. I kept screaming. No words at first, just cries and groans.

Then, a voice. It was mine. "Jesus! I can't do this," loud at first, then quieter, "Do something," I sobbed. "Help me. Please help me," I was crying. "Take this pain. Please."

A hand touched my shoulder. I jerked my head, looking for a nurse, a doctor, someone standing there. I was alone. And the pain was gone. It had not eased or lessened. It was gone. I lay staring at the ceiling. Nurses came and wheeled my bed through two large swinging doors. Surgery. Hands grasped the bed sheet corners and gently slid me onto a wider table. I shut my eyes against large overhead lights. I felt no pain. Nothing. I closed my eyes as sleep mercifully came.

I was rudely awakened by a man shouting in my face, "CHRISTINE! DO YOU KNOW WHAT DAY THIS IS?"

Shut up, I thought to myself. Still, the voice, "CHRISTINE! DO YOU KNOW WHERE YOU ARE?"

Was he ever going to shut up? "Yes," my voice came slowly up from somewhere dark, a deep, crackling sound, still weak.

"WHERE ARE YOU CHRISTINE?"

So loud. Be quiet. "Hospital," I whispered, traveling back.

"WHY ARE YOU HERE CHRISTINE?"

"Pregnancy. Surgery."

"Okay, that's good," this time a gentler sound, softer. "How are you feeling?"

I don't know, I thought, but did not speak it aloud.

He checked some tubes poking out of my arm, scrutinized the bleeping sounds coming from the monitors over my head, and smiled at me. He lifted my hand, turned it over to examine the palm, studying each finger. "Someone will be in soon to give you a sponge bath."

I lifted my hands closer to my face. There was dried blood between each finger, under my fingernails, and streaks left on my forearms. I was to find out later that the surgeon's first incision erupted in copious amounts of blood spewing and spraying.

"Your husband is here," he said as he left the room.

Instantly it seemed, Danny came through the door and was at my bedside. He held my hand.

"There's no more baby," I said.

"I know," he said. "It's okay, it's okay," he squeezed my hand tight. "I love you."

We both cried.

For this cause shall a man leave his father and mother, and cleave to his wife. And they twain shall be one flesh; so then they are no more twain, but one flesh. What therefore God hath joined together, let not man put asunder. Mark 10:7-9, KJV

The Hebrew word for 'joined' is 'opposites.'

MADISON HEIGHTS, MICHIGAN

1966 - 1970

CHAPTER ONE

———⊶⊷———

The evil thing may originate in the malignity of a Judas;
but by the time it reaches us it has become the cup which
our Father has given us to drink.

F.B. Meyer

Our wedding day dawned sunny with not one cloud to eclipse an azure blue sky. It was beautiful. The 80 degree temperature was tempered by a soft breeze. The imposing and somewhat gothic appearance of the church with its massive oak doors, stained glass windows and towering spiral only added to the day's solemnity. All my child-like prayers were about to be played out as I took my first step down the aisle to become Mrs. Daniel Pechacek. So real in my dreams had been the journey I was about to embark upon, the day felt like the opening act of a play I had rehearsed endlessly. I had this role down to perfection.

A Catholic wedding ceremony is formal and packed with enough grandeur to inspire awe in the most jaded of souls. At that most reverent point in the ceremony when bride, groom, best man and maid-of-honor all kneel to receive communion, it happened. I knelt on the padded portable kneeler, one of four set up for the wedding party at the altar, directly in front of the priest. With my back ramrod straight and my hands folded prayerfully, I listened attentively as Father Farell prepared the Sacrament. In a matter of seconds, his voice changed to a distant buzzing sound. I leaned in closer but the buzzing became louder. My vision blurred. A part of my brain told me what was happening but the rest of me did not seem to care. I slowly slumped forward, my head hanging over the arm support of my personal kneeler. I was quietly on my way to becoming a heap of white lace and hoop skirt on the floor at the feet of Father Farell, giving our guests full view of my lacy undergarments.

Danny grabbed my arm. My head and shoulders continued the downward spiral. Despite my best efforts, my vision faded to tiny black specks. Danny held firmly to my arm and pulled me back to an upright position with as much dignity as possible given that I was a limp mound of frothy white satin and lace.

"Are you all right?" Father Farell's voice echoed from a distant place. Images slowly returned as the dark began to recede.

"I don't think so," I whispered. He signaled the altar boys to retrieve a chair for the fading bride. I gratefully sat, slumped over like a rag doll. So as to spare me the humiliation of being the only person sitting, chairs were provided for all four of us during the communion portion of the ceremony. While being the center of attention on this special day was certainly my goal, being flat on my face before an audience, hoop skirt in the air, out cold was not part of my plan.

Following the church ceremony and my most humiliating decline at the altar, the guests, consisting of scarce family members and fewer friends, gathered together at a small block building located in the city of Memphis for the wedding breakfast. After the meal, people drifted outside. The two camps of family members circled, marking territory, keeping a safe distance from the opposing family. The Pechacek Camp and the Wener Camp. Like the proverbial Hatfields and McCoys, each family stood their ground and in the middle stood the bride and groom. It was brief and awkward. The people in attendance did not want to spend any more time in present company than absolutely necessary.

Following the fleeting, strained get-together, we headed back to the house in Memphis where I currently resided with Danny's mother, Milly, to change our wedding clothes and leave for the honeymoon. The first order of business was opening wedding gifts. I lingered, not wanting to get out of my wedding gown. This would be the one and only time I would wear this beautiful gown and I wanted to enjoy it as long as possible. The veil, not so much.

"Are you ready to change so we can get out of here?" my new husband asked. I sensed he was done with smiling and making polite conversation.

"Okay, give me a minute," I said.

Our bags were packed and in the car, ready to go. I changed into the first dress of my trousseau. It was a white cotton shirtwaist dress, with tiny blue cornflowers covering the material. Small pearl buttons went from waist to neck, where a petite white peter-pan collar set. It had short cap sleeves and a thin blue belt at the waist. The skirt was full and fell just at my knees. It was feminine and delicate, swinging and brushing softly against my thighs as I walked. I had not owned a dress like it before. I was a married woman.

I had boundaries now, a future with a name to it, a purpose that did not depend on the chaos going on around me. I believed that this day marked a new beginning and just as I had put on a new dress, I had put on a new life. My naiveté at eighteen years old convinced me that it was possible to close the chapter on the past and begin anew.

Changed and packed, I walked out the front door and headed to our car, a blue on blue 1961 Pontiac Bonneville, where my husband waited. Just steps from the door, arms grabbed me from behind and dragged me to a waiting car. Like vultures circling an unguarded nest, the groomsmen had lain in wait as I changed into more suitable clothing for a kidnapping.

"Danny!" I screamed.

He turned in time to see me thrust into the back seat of a car. The door slammed shut and we sped away. I looked out the back window to see Danny making a fast but futile attempt to chase the car. The look on his face was not a happy one. My captors drove aimlessly for forty-five minutes, laughing uproariously, pleased with their triumph of outwitting the groom. As the stolen treasure, I was not laughing.

My earlier assessment of Danny's reaction to the frivolity of his friends had been correct. He was not amused. Finally returning me once again and after several minutes of hand shaking and forced laughter, we got into our car to leave. Dan, still smiling, turned the key in the ignition. The engine strained and choked. Danny's already pushed to the limit temper threatened to erupt. It had been a long day. Fatigue and stress settled over both of us and the desire to be gone was burning. After several failed attempts to start the engine, Danny got out, lifted the hood, and found rags packed into and around the air cleaner. The male members of our wedding party convulsed into a fresh bout of laughter. Back behind the wheel, Dan gave his friends a strained, tight-lipped smile, started the engine and drove us away.

Our honeymoon was one week spent traveling through Canada. Before crossing the Blue Water Bridge and passing from the United States into Canada, we spent our first night as husband and wife at a small motel in the city of Port Huron, Michigan.

The motel was typical of motels in 1966. The rooms, twelve in all, made a horseshoe around a paved parking lot which bordered the highway. The motel office was located in the middle of the horseshoe. We told no one where we planned to spend our first night as husband and wife.

The drive to Port Huron from Memphis was quiet. We were exhausted and ready to be alone. After forty-five minutes Dan pulled into our motel parking lot.

As Danny shut off the ignition, he turned to me and said, "I'll go in and get a room." I was shaking. I had never been in a motel room before and certainly not with a man.

"What if the clerk thinks we aren't married?" I whispered.

"What?" Danny said and laughed. "So what?"

I had no answer to that and left the situation up to my husband, confident he knew best. I stayed in the car, attempting to keep out of sight, just in case the prying eyes of the motel clerk would look my way. For one moment of panic, I wondered if this stranger would demand to see proof that we were indeed married. Did we bring our marriage license, I wondered. I was both nervous and embarrassed. Now a married woman, eager to be world-wise and confident in my new status, I could not escape my own innocence and timidity. Every step of this new life from here on would be firsts and I was eager to appear smart and sophisticated for my new husband, as he certainly appeared to me.

In truth, neither one of us were smart or sophisticated.

Our honeymoon was perfect as far as I was concerned. We spent five wonderful days alone together. I was married to the love of my life, pregnant with our first child, and ready to begin our life together. What could go wrong?

CHAPTER TWO

———⋘⋙———

Love has nothing to do with what you are expecting to get,
only what you are expecting to give, which is everything.
                                              Katherine Hepburn

We easily settled into our new lives as a married couple. Danny was employed as a Sheet Metal apprentice and worked for E. W. Evans Sheet Metal in Ferndale. I was a wife and homemaker. And in just a few short months we would become parents.

Our first days at 30204 Barrington in Madison Heights were a flurry of unpacking and organizing. The house, a two bedroom bungalow, was small, encompassing just over 700 square feet of living space with no basement and no garage. We had purchased the house earlier in the year and Dan lived in it alone until we married. All of my meager paychecks earned at Bud's Meat Market and Bakery during my senior year of high school went to build up a savings we used for a down payment on a house. It never occurred to either of us to rent a house or an apartment. Danny had counted on, and planned for, the purchase of a house and I did not question his decision or ability to make it happen. I deferred to him in all things.

As a young child I had learned to be compliant, seeking to please by my willingness to be agreeable. My behavior was predicated on my belief that if I did not complain or cause dissent, life went smoothly and according to plan. This was going to be the perfect marriage and in order for that to happen, I must first be the perfect wife. My definition of a perfect wife was to be nothing like my mother, who had lost her husband to another woman, and certainly not like my step-mother, who had been the other woman.

Immediately after our honeymoon, we went to Milly's house on Boardman Road in Memphis to pack up my remaining belongings and to collect the wedding presents. Our wedding had fallen just two weeks prior to my high school graduation. The original plan was to return in time for me to participate in the graduation ceremony. While on our honeymoon, I decided I did not want to go through the actual graduation ceremony. Danny agreed and instead of rushing back, we lingered a day longer and returned late into the evening of the graduation.

We failed to get word to Milly of our change in plans, and so she, my sister, Shirley Ann, and Danny's sister, Teresa, all went to the graduation ceremony. Returning home afterwards, she found Danny and me sitting on the couch together. Her anger was immediate.

"Where were you?" she said. I had been here before and knew better than to respond. Silently I prepared myself for the inevitable backlash of actions taken independent of the defined order under her rule.

When Milly's anger erupted, any questions she might utter were rhetorical. The clipped words were stated to accuse, judge the offender's actions, and announce judgment on the condemned. A defense was not expected and never considered.

"We just got back a little while ago," I said.

"Well, you were supposed to be at graduation," she spat. "I was left just to sit there. It was embarrassing."

Married though I may be, I was scolded like an errant child. My new husband sat silent, not venturing to speak a word in our defense. He dared not stand up to his mother. He was a man with a wife now, responsible for building our lives together; but, Milly held as tightly to him at that moment as she had in the past. As we sat under her stare, I knew not many things had changed. Milly was still a force to be reckoned with and it would not matter how far away we lived, she would rule our lives. In that moment it became glaringly clear to me that I could not expect, nor would receive, support from my new husband in matters involving his mother, my now mother-in-law.

I tried to look contrite as the tirade continued. It was wiser to look attentive and wait it out. With one last accusatory look our way, Milly turned her back on us and walked away.

Once we escaped the powerful laser rays of Milly's universe, we traveled to our own home in Madison Heights. The space consisted of two small bedrooms, a close-quartered bathroom, living room with a large picture window, a kitchen and laundry room. The kitchen now filled with refrigerator, table, chairs and cook stove, left just enough room to maneuver. The narrow laundry room held a used washer and dryer, the furnace and a back door. Bending over in the tiny space required turning your body sideways from the washer and dryer to avoid bumping into the wall.

Most of our furnishings were hand-me-downs. We were grateful to have them. Our bedroom furniture, two dressers, one large mirror and headboard were new, purchased with money Danny received from an auto accident. Just three months before our wedding a drunk driver ran into the rear panel of the Bonneville. Dan decided he could repair the spot himself and keep the insurance money. The resulting self-repair was a large blob of gray matter slathered over the crunched fender and covered with duct tape. He did not bother to paint the result of his handiwork but was nevertheless proud of his repair job. I was excited that we could now have a brand new bedroom set. The insurance money covered the cost of the furniture but left nothing for a mattress set. As was Dan's firm bent, we purchased nothing on credit. We would save up money for a mattress. Unfortunately, that did not meet our immediate need. Joe, Danny's father, offered to give us the double mattress that Dan had slept on during the time he lived with him. We gratefully accepted.

The mattress, of indeterminate age, sagged in the middle, resulting in snuggling, intended or not. My preferred sleeping style was to wrap myself around Dan like a wild vine. He preferred some breathing room. But the slump in the middle gave him little choice. The mattress served its purpose until one morning I awakened to discover a bloody slash of unknown origin on my hip. A rogue spring had popped through the fabric of the mattress puncturing my skin. Not long after we were able to purchase a new mattress. By this time, my new husband enjoyed being vined.

Once Danny returned to work and I was left doing the everyday things concerning being a wife, it afforded me time to become acquainted with some of our neighbors. The husbands all left the neighborhood around the same time each morning, leaving wives and children at home. As young wives, most near my age, we were not long out of high school. And in many respects the women of the neighborhood approached life much the same as they had in high school.

Barrington Street had clicks, or groups of Who's Who. Entrance into, or exiting out of, any one of the groups was arbitrary and decided upon by the rules of the neighborhood. I am uncertain who decided upon the rules or what the rules actually were, but they existed. As in high school, if you became friends one day with someone then you were automatically not friends with someone else. The reasons were varied and many, all supported by gossipy tales. Tidbits were exchanged over coffee at one house where you sat for one or two hours of each day talking and supporting your gossip with imaginary facts, all necessary to be included in whichever circle you happened to be in at the time.

It became a full time job. You dare not take a day off for fear of becoming the object of derision, ostracized from the group. Everyone was a best friend while sitting at your table drinking bad coffee, smoking cigarettes, and sharing deep confidences, which the day before and around a different kitchen table, had been told along with an oath never to reveal them to another soul. House to house we went, day after day, building our little kingdom. As part of our entertainment we formed card clubs. Pinochle was a favorite among the group. I was asked to join the group and eagerly accepted. I did not know how to play Pinochle but learned. Unfortunately, no one had invited me to play Euchre, a card game at which I was adept. Pinochle involved several players, which meant more ladies around the table, resulting in more gossip to pass on, digest and store away for future discussion.

It was a feather in your cap to be invited and to refuse was unthinkable. We did not play once a week during the day; although, we certainly seemed to have an excessive amount of free time, which we spent drinking coffee and gossiping. Instead, we all gathered at someone's house in the evening, leaving husband and children alone while we gossiped, smoked cigarettes, drank bad coffee, occasionally substituting sodas for coffee, and wrapped it all in the guise of playing cards. These rituals were not so much a desire to be included in the group to make new friends as they were the dread of being outside the group and served up as the sacrificial goat for future gatherings. I joined in with as much gossip as the next. I refrained however, from talking about my sex life with the group. I held firmly to the belief that it was private, intimate and no one else's business.

Unfortunately, it did not remain so.

CHAPTER THREE

Experience, that most brutal of teachers.
But you learn, my God do you learn.

C.S. Lewis

Our daughter arrived five weeks earlier than planned or predicted by my doctor. From that moment and into adulthood, it remains the one and only time Julie has made an early arrival.

Shortly after settling in as a married couple, I sought out an obstetrician. We wanted the pregnancy confirmed in order to announce a date of arrival. It must be a respectable length of time after we were married. Never mind that when the actual birth occurred, it would be obvious that I had been pregnant at our wedding. And I was hoping for some relief from my constant nausea and repeated vomiting. My morning sickness seemed to have morphed into all my waking hours. My toilet bowl was bleach-clean every day. There were no odors or spots. This was not due to a particular affinity or obsession with clean bathrooms. It was because every day, sometimes several times a day, my head went down into the toilet bowl, giving up whatever it was I had attempted to consume that day. If I was to be on intimate terms with my toilet bowl, it was going to be clean.

One of my new neighbors gave me the name of an obstetrician and I made my initial appointment for the coming week. That weekend Danny drove the route to the doctor's office in order to point the way for me. I was an inexperienced driver, having had my license less than three years and had never driven in the kind of traffic that was Woodward Avenue. Thinking about traveling alone on busy city streets caused me enough anxiety that I spent a great deal of time thinking of ways to get out of the whole event. But, as I realized late one night contemplating labor and delivery, you simply cannot decide to not show up.

Just three months out of high school, I was not far removed from the same anxieties that had plagued me during my growing up years. Fear of the unknown continued to gnaw at me like a nagging tooth ache you try to ignore. If I was careful not to chomp down on anything out of my comfort zone, I managed to forget it was there. But married life was proving to be one giant abscess. Growing up silent was the safest way to be in our house. As I grew older, I saw no reason to veer from this plan. People assumed my behavior was confidence, even snobbery. In reality, I did not want people to find out the truth. I was ashamed that at eighteen years old, married, and pregnant, I was afraid—of everything. The dark. Being alone. Not being accepted. That I was unattractive. Not smart. Worst of all, and perhaps the most insidious, self-destructive lie, was that my young, handsome, charming husband was better than me and had perhaps married beneath him.

Months before, when I told Danny in hushed whispers that I might be pregnant, we knew it had to be confirmed. Because Helen Gurley-Brown had not yet liberated young women with the freedom of public, frequent, indiscriminate sexual encounters, multiple sexual partners, and the opportunity to be totally irresponsible, being pregnant out of wedlock was still kept private. The feminist movement headed by Gloria Steinem, with its marches and cries of freedom for poor unfortunate, enslaved women, (of which apparently I was an ignorant member) was in its early stages.

16

Drug store shelves were not yet lined with home pregnancy tests for the set-free, liberated woman.

Danny's uncle, John Pechacek, was a general practitioner in Warren, not far from the flat Danny then shared with his father, Joe. We went to his office one Saturday soon after our whispered conversation. I supplied the requisite urine sample. John supplied the news. I was indeed pregnant.

We were euphoric. I cried and laughed, hardly believing that a new life was growing inside me, a life that Danny and I had created. Danny grinned. We wondered if this would be a boy or a girl. And we talked about names. I wanted the name Daniel, if the baby turned out to be a boy.

"I've always imagined having a boy first, brown hair and brown eyes. Like you," I said.

"Well, if it's a girl," Danny said, "I want to name her Julie."

"Really?" I asked. "Any particular reason?"

"No," he said. "I've just always liked that name. I think it's a pretty name."

I was not particularly fond of that name and did not know anyone with that name. But, as always, I agreed with whatever my husband said.

"Okay. Julie is a pretty name." I thought no more of it, convinced I would be giving birth to a boy.

My Doctor set my due date for January 12th, still somewhat shy of a respectful nine months. We announced a February due date to family and friends. Julie arrived on the sixth of December at 10:30 p.m.

My labor began quietly. I was not certain that the low back pain nagging at me was actually labor. My perception of labor was based on tales told by my new neighbors. I tried not to think of that. The books I read failed to paint a clear picture. And so, when I awoke with a backache, I dismissed it. Dan was at work. I was home alone. Alone, except for the in-and-out of the usual neighbors.

The morning turned to afternoon and still, this backache would not go away. In fact, it had come full circle and now encompassed my abdomen. And, the ache seemed to be at regular intervals.

Sharon, another neighbor, popped in for coffee late in the afternoon. "What's up?" she asked.

"I've kind of been lying around," I said. "I'm not feeling too well."

"Really?" Sharon's eyes opened like rocket after burners. "Like how?"

"I'm tense," I said. Almost involuntarily my hands went to my pregnant belly.

"You're in labor, aren't you?" She stared at me like a starving person eyeing a hot, tender roast beef.

"No," I said, dismissing the idea. "I can't be. I have six more weeks to go." This I said hopefully.

"I better take you to the hospital," Sharon said and jumped up, heading for the door.

"No, I'll wait for Danny."

"He might not get home in time," Sharon urged.

I was suddenly more than nervous. "I can call the shop and make sure he comes right home," I told her. Sharon grabbed the phone and shoved it at me.

"Hi Mr. Evans," I said, "This is Chris Pechacek. Is Dan still there?"

"No, he just left," he said. "Is everything all right?"

"Well, I think I'm in labor," I said.

"He's dropping Bob Dudley off at home," he said. "Call there. You might catch him."

I hung up and dialed the Dudley's. Sharon stood hovering over me. Mrs. Dudley assured me that the minute Danny appeared in the driveway she would send him on his way.

As Dan pulled in the driveway, her head came out the front door and she shouted, "Dan get home! Right now! You wife is in labor!"

Sharon stayed with me until Danny walked through the door. I was relieved to see my husband. I felt safer now and decidedly less afraid. Sharon was disappointed.

"Damn," Sharon said. "I've always wanted to drive someone in labor to the hospital."

There had been no need for urgency. We arrived at Beaumont Hospital in Oak Park a short time later, entering through the emergency doors. I was whisked away in a wheel chair while a nurse corralled Danny to her desk for the insurance information. He turned to watch as I disappeared down a hallway. The nurse took his arm and said, "You'll see your wife in just a few minutes." Smiling, she added, "She'll be fine."

Danny did see me in a short while, but there had been no reason to rush. Undressed, put into bed, I was sitting up and waiting. The nurse and doctor arrived to examine me.

"Things are progressing nicely, Mr. Pechacek," he assured Danny. "Why don't you wait for a bit in the waiting room? It's more comfortable."

Danny did wait in the father's waiting room. Other than intermittent visits to my bedside, which was all that was allowed at the time, he waited forty-four hours. He sat, paced, smoked and sat some more. Having no money in his pocket, payday was four days away, he could not even buy a cup of coffee. Another soon-to-be dad noticed Dan by the rumbling of his by now empty stomach.

"Hey, when did you eat last," he laughed.

"Oh, I'm fine," Dan said casually. Growl-rumble.

"Let me give you a couple of bucks," he offered. "Go to the cafeteria and get a bite. They'll call you when it's time."

"No, but thanks. I'm fine," Dan said again. Growl.

"Listen, here's two bucks. Take it," the man insisted and pushed two one dollar bills at Dan.

"Thanks," Danny said as he accepted the money. He walked to the cafeteria and bought one hamburger and a coffee. Walking back to the waiting room, he could not remember chewing the burger. The noise in his stomach was quiet. And now, forty-six years later, he carries a folded twenty dollar bill tucked away in his wallet for emergencies.

Julie Marie Pechacek arrived on December 6, 1966. Screaming, healthy, red hair, and weighing 7 pounds and 6 ounces, she would not pass for a baby due in February. We remained mute on the issue.

After my required four day stay in the hospital, Danny arrived to take his new daughter and wife home. Julie slept in a borrowed bassinette next to our bed. The first night was difficult for both mother and daughter. I was frightened and exhausted. Near dawn, we both fell asleep. Later in the morning, Julie began to stir. As I contemplated forcing my tired eyes open, the bedroom door opened and Dan came quietly to the bassinette. I peered out from heavy lids as he leaned over our newborn daughter.

"Good morning sweetheart," he whispered. "Let's let Mommy sleep. You come with Daddy." Danny reached down into the bassinette and carried our daughter to another room. He changed her diaper, warmed a bottle and fed her. Father and daughter sat together in the rocking chair until Julie fell asleep.

I opted to bottle feed my daughter. I regret that choice. The decision was made out of part ignorance, part youth, and a great deal of peer pressure. The new friends I had made during the short span of my married life did not breastfeed their infants and thought the whole process was crude. I believe much of the negative attitudes surrounding the natural, nutritious and beautiful art of breastfeeding stemmed from the growing feminist storm gaining momentum in United States during this time. Even on tiny Barrington Street, the clouds hovered. Breastfeeding tied a woman down and caused her to be subjected to something akin to servant-hood, or so we were told. The breast was a mark of weakness. Women burned bras and refused to wear the contraption that was apparently now a metaphor for being bound to a man in slavery. Going braless was not something I embraced. It was both unattractive and painful.

While I did not adhere to the tenets of the new movement that had come to set me free from a trap I was unaware existed, I was subject to peer pressure. The thoughts and ideas of those around me ruled my life. I had yet to learn who I was as a person or that a separate me actually existed somewhere buried beneath the refuse of my growing up.

CHAPTER FOUR

———∽∾∽———

Husbands are like tattoos—you should wait until you come across
something you want on your body for the rest of your life.
                                                    Sloane Crosley

Barrington Street was one block long. The seven houses sitting
on the short street were close together. Each lot was 60x120 feet.
Our house set at one end of the block, which angled into another
street, making our backyard larger than the yards of our neighbors. Every front yard was the same; small, cropped with a brief
concrete walkway leading to two steps ending at a small porch.
What made our backyard unique, other than its larger size, were
the numerous fruit trees and flowering smaller trees. The previous
owners apparently loved fruit and flowers.

The Culpeppers, an elderly couple who previously lived in our
home had moved back to Tennessee. They had, for some time,
neglected to prune, trim, or tend to, the vegetation growing in
the yard. The trees had produced little fruit. Neither Danny nor
I knew about garden husbandry and had little interest in learning. The yard exhibited our lack of interest. Wayward branches,

fallen fruit, and leaves littered the yard. The simple task of mowing became an exercise in working through an obstacle course.

"I'm going to trim those trees once and for all," Dan said one Saturday morning. He was on his way out to mow the lawn.

"Trim or chop down?" I asked. Danny had threatened to clear-cut the yard on more than one occasion after spending the day raking, trimming, picking up brush, and hauling the debris to the vacant lot across the street.

"I'm not sure," he murmured. Dan's expression told me he was already out in the yard like Paul Bunyan, axe in hand, with Babe the Blue Ox at his side.

"It's up to you," I said. "I don't care one way or the other."

I had cursed the trees myself more than once. My dryer was the clothesline that ran the length of the back yard. Taking clothes off the line only to have them littered with leaves, buds, and green flying things was frustrating. Besides, it would be nice to see my neighbor's yards without branches to block my view. One neighbor in particular especially needed watching; a fact I discovered much too late.

"Yeah, I'm going to take my hand saw and do some trimming,"

Danny spent the entire day cutting, trimming, and chopping. By late afternoon, the middle of the yard was stacked with the remnants of fruit trees, shrubs, and anything else that threatened to bud, grow, or shed. The result resembled a crude shelter. It stood five feet high and twelve feet in circumference.

"Wow," I said as I came out the back door. The massive mound was impressive. I had been busy in the house for the better part of the day and other than an occasional glance out the window, when the odd expletive sailed through the air, I kept out of the way.

"Honey, that is more than a trim," I said.

"It is, isn't it," he said. He looked at the pile as though noticing it for the first time.

"What are you going to do with it now?" I asked. We both stared at the mountain of debris before us. It brought to mind a fort, built for retreating into the nether regions of a dark, foreboding forest.

"You can't possibly haul all that over to the vacant lot," I remarked. "Somebody will notice that."

The vacant lot across the street was the neighborhood depository for lawn clippings and shrub trimmings. I was fairly certain anyone with a keen eye would take note of trimmings that reached greater heights than the miniature mounds usually deposited on a Saturday afternoon. This thing looked like a squatter's new residence, one big enough for a family.

"I guess I'll have to burn it," he said more to himself than me.

"Burn it?" I was getting worried. "All at once?" I asked.

"Well of course," he now focused on me like I had just landed on planet earth. "What else do you think I'm going to do with all this," he said as his arm swept over the expanse.

"Okay," I shrugged and went back in the house. "You're making a big mistake," I muttered as I walked away.

The pile standing in the middle of our back yard resembled the makings of a bonfire ready to begin the celebration for homecoming at a college football game. It most certainly did not look like the kind of fire you lit to take care of errant yard debris, in a crowded neighborhood, on a quiet Saturday afternoon, while families relaxed and children played. I went inside to make certain the baby stayed away from any windows.

As Dan stood, leaning on the rake handle, chin resting on his hands, George Allen appeared. George, Sharon's husband, was tall, slender, dark haired, and quiet. He worked as a draftsman at a nearby factory and other than seeing him on weekends, George kept to himself. He and Dan had developed a friendship.

"Hey Dan," George said as he came into the backyard. He walked over to stand next to Danny. They both now stared at the pile.

"Hi George," Dan answered.

"What are you doing?" George did not take his eyes off the pile.

"I cleaned up the yard," Danny told him.

"What are you going to do with all this?"

"I need to burn it," Danny answered.

"Uh-huh," was George's contribution to the idea.

"Just figuring out where to start."

"Burn the whole thing at one time," George said. "Put some gasoline on it first so it'll start hot and fast," he suggested. "You want it to burn and stay burning until it's all gone."

"Yeah, that's a good idea," Dan agreed. He turned to retrieve the gasoline can he kept in the small shed at the back of the yard. It was full.

Danny came back to his Paul Bunyan mound of highly flammable brush, took the cap off the gas can and did a few sweeps with the can, sprinkling on one side. He lit a match, threw it into the pile and jumped back. Nothing. He lit another match, threw it on the wood. Nothing. Frowning, he knelt closer to the woodpile, lit another match, held it closer this time and waited. Nothing.

George sprang into action. "Give me that," he grabbed the gas can. "You need to put more gas on it." Holding the can high, he let gas sail over the top of the wood. He circled the expanse of the wood pile, hurling gasoline as he went, until the can was empty.

Danny stood watching. Finally, George came back to stand next to Danny. "You think that might be too much," Danny wondered.

"Naw," George shook his head as he spoke. He reached for the matches. "You want it to burn down, don't you?"

The next 30 seconds was either heart-stopping terror or the stuff of which movies are made. Your viewpoint depended on your immediate proximity to what happened and whether you fled for your life or stood awe-struck by the awesome display.

George pulled one match from the pack and said to Dan, "We better stand back a little, just in case." They both backed away from the pile a respectable distance.

Scrrraach. . . the match slid across the matchbook flap.

Hisssss. . .the tiny flame sprang up.

George threw the match onto the pile.

BOOM! A four foot wave of fire rose up from the outer ridge of the woodpile. It encircled the entire circumference of the mound in less than two seconds. It belched outward. Dan and George jumped out and up simultaneously, in a narrow escape; the wall of flames missing their feet by inches. Both men lunged backwards, tripping as they went.

The windows of not just our house, but surrounding houses, thundered to almost breaking. The boom echoed over to the next street. The elderly couple living directly behind us, and sitting at their picnic table observing, fled. The speed with which they disappeared into their house belied their advanced years. The neighbors to our left stood dumb-struck with impending doom.

I ran to the back door, clutching Julie and stared. The heat from the flames penetrated the closed door. The pile was now a monstrous ball of fire rocketing some 50 feet in the air. Neighbors cautiously crept outside once again after having fled in terror. They hunched low, ready to flee for cover, as they made their way to stare in disbelief at the spectacle in our yard.

Laughing, Danny and George stared at one another, each with singed hair, eyebrows, and lashes.

"DAMN!" Danny shouted.

"DAMN!" George echoed.

They both stood watching the blaze, which was beginning to calm to an even flame. It was still high and dangerous looking, but coming under control.

"Are you okay," Danny asked.

"Sure," George said as he felt his face and scratched at what was left of his eyebrows. "Didn't I tell you that would work?"

CHAPTER FIVE

———— ∞∞∞ ————

An appeaser is someone who feeds the alligator,
hoping it will eat him last.

Winston Churchill

Married life settled into a happy routine. Danny continued his sheet metal apprenticeship with E.W.Evans & Company. I was doing what I had always dreamed, being Danny's wife, keeping our little house and most recently being a new mom. Danny left each weekday morning, lunch pail fully packed, and arrived back home by 5 p.m. and every evening at 6 p.m., we sat at our tiny Formica-topped table for dinner.

I had not done much cooking as a teenager. As a result, my culinary skills were limited. The scant number of meals in my repertoire was adequate but not creative. As it turned out, my narrow scope of meal preparation worked to our advantage. Danny's weekly net pay of $63 and change was budgeted to cover our monthly bills, spending money, groceries and a portion to a savings account. A twenty-dollar bill went into a sock drawer each week to cover our monthly house payment of $79 and Dan kept eight dollars for spending money. His allowance covered cigarettes, thirty-five cents a pack and gasoline, twenty-seven cents a gallon. My weekly grocery allowance stayed within ten to fifteen dollars. I was not an exploratory cook so staying within a budget was easily accomplished. It took the guess work out of meal planning. We ate well. Our used Kelvinator refrigerator was never empty and neither were our stomachs.

My cooking was predictable. My firm belief was that a boring routine was preferable to attempting the untried, which may result in failure; or worse, criticism from my husband. My entry into married life might have been eager, wholehearted, even blind, but it left no room for mistakes.

One rule of Catholicism was no meat on Fridays. The reason for the edict was a mystery to me, but I dutifully obeyed with no questions asked. Fish was an option, but I did not know how to cook fish nor did I know where to go and purchase fresh fish. I stuck to basics. If eating meat on a Friday was going to send me to Hell, then I would not cook or eat meat on Friday. My life to this point was either/or. There was one straight path to follow, with no tributaries for exploration. The no-meat-eating Friday was not something Danny and I discussed, as were most subjects. I remained silent; fearful of stepping over an arbitrary line bringing displeasure from God, or more importantly, my new, handsome husband, who, I remained convinced, had married beneath his station in life.

The cost of our Friday meal was an economical marvel. Each Friday I purchased one box of Chef Boyardee Spaghetti. For twenty-nine cents, the box contained a bag of noodles, one can of sauce with cheese, no meat, and one packet of parmesan cheese. To accompany this culinary delight, I prepared one box of Jiffy Corn Muffins, which cost ten cents, and yielded six muffins. Our total Friday night dinner cost thirty-nine cents. This meal was served every Friday night. If Danny thought the meal tedious, he never brought the matter to my attention.

By our first Thanksgiving together my confidence as a culinary had evolved to such a level that I boldly decided to cook my first turkey dinner. I purchased a frozen ten-pounder. Per the directions that I found printed on the soggy paper tucked in with the turkey, the magnificent bird set in a sink of cool water for two days defrosting. Early Thanksgiving morning I was in my kitchen, with a brand new apron on, the sashes tied in a perfect bow, the ends hanging saucily down my backside, eager to put the bird in the oven. Staring down at the unwrapped, floppy bird in the sink, I envisioned serving a golden brown delectable feast to the amazement of all attending, one worthy of a Norman Rockwell painting. Jilted back to reality by the naked bird in my sink, I realized that other than putting it in a roaster and in the oven, I had no idea how to proceed. I called my neighbor, Mary.

"Hi Mary," I said. "I'm cooking a turkey. What do I do?"

"Have you ever cooked one before?" Mary laughed.

"No, but it can't be that hard."

"Okay, first rinse out the inside really good," she explained. "And then take the giblets. You'll need to boil them for gravy."

"The what?" I was looking inside the turkey but all I saw was pink skin and frozen chunks.

"The giblets," Mary repeated. "The neck, gizzard, heart and liver."

I made a gagging sound. "That's disgusting. Why do I want all that?"

"Boiling those makes for a very nice gravy base," she said. "And, trust me they taste good."

I did not believe her but dutifully dug inside the turkey cavity for the offending items.

"There's nothing in here," I said as I peered closely inside the dead turkey.

"Are you sure? They should be there in a small paper-like sack."

"Mary, this bird is not that big and there is no place to hide." I stressed. "Just tell me what to do about stuffing."

Mary gave me a detailed recipe over the phone for stuffing. I followed her steps to the letter resulting in moist, flavorful stuffing. For the next several years, early each Thanksgiving morning, I called Mary for the same recipe and we walked through it as we talked. It became as much a holiday tradition as baking Christmas cookies.

By day's end, the turkey was baked to a stunning golden brown. I proudly served it along with mashed potatoes, stuffing, and several other traditional Thanksgiving delights. As we sat around the table, Dan stood to do the honors of slicing the first pieces of turkey. On the second cut, a tiny white bag fell from the front of the bird. Dan poked at it with the knife and out fell a neck, gizzard, heart and liver.

"Oh, that's where that was."

Christmas time surprised both Dan and me, not because it came as scheduled on the twenty-fifth of December, but because we did not anticipate Julie's arrival until after the holidays. Her early arrival caused me to re-evaluate my planned traditional festivities; sending out Christmas cards, baking cookies, buying and wrapping gifts and of utmost importance purchasing a Christmas tree from a snow covered lot.

Dan and I both remembered the tree buying events from our childhood as important and exciting. Our families may have been fractured, even crazy but for at least one evening a year, a semblance of sanity prevailed long enough for the perfect tree to be chosen, purchased and brought home to be decorated with lights, bulbs and tinsel. The glittery tinsel was my favorite part of the tree decorations, and the thicker the better. I loved the way each silvery strand moved and sparkled. Unfortunately, Dan did not share my passion for tinsel. Had there been a move to ban its sale or distribution, my husband would be the first to vote in the affirmative.

"Chris, I find that stuff all over the house," he announced. "Stop putting it on so thick. I'll be picking those damn silver things out of my hair." I opined that he was exaggerating, but in the end his irrational dislike of the beautiful gossamer shreds prevailed.

Julie's early arrival threw our timing off but did not cancel plans. Just days before Christmas Eve with our newborn daughter bundled up, we drove to the Sears store on 15 Mile Road and John R. It was bitter cold and the snow crunched as we walked across the parking lot to the store entrance. Loudspeakers carried Christmas carols and strings of colored lights adorned light poles, doors and windows. Dan carried Julie, wrapped all in pink against the cold in one arm, and with the other, he held onto me. Inside the store, Dan uncovered Julie's face. Her eyes, wide and wondering, reflected the glow of the lights.

We had a Christmas list. It was a brief list because we had little money to spend. Once the allotted amount set aside for gifts was gone, we were finished shopping. Limiting our purchases to our cash reserve was a practice set at our first Christmas and has never varied over our forty-seven Christmases together.

From Sears we drove to a tree lot near our house. Dan masterfully examined tree after tree in the snow covered rows. Occasionally he paused, pulled one tree from the bunch, turned it around, examined its trunk and slammed it down on the frozen ground. I was uncertain why this was done but my father had done the same thing so it must be Christmas tree buying savvy. After several thumps of various trees, we choose the perfect one. Dan tied our tree to the top of the car and we drove home. The tree set outside until the next day when it could be examined more thoroughly in the daylight. Satisfied that this was a perfect choice and once decorated with hand-me-down decorations, it would be a magnificent sight.

The next evening, dinner over and Julie asleep in her crib, Dan brought the tree inside our small living room and laid it on a sheet spread over the carpet. The heavy snow was melted and the branches now fell majestically, waiting for strings of bright lights. Dan lifted the tree to set its trunk in the stand. It did not fit. Pulling it out once more, he examined the bottom more closely.

"The trunk is too wide," he said. "I'll have to get my saw and trim it." Dan retrieved his saw from our shed, came back inside and began to cut away. It was still too wide for the stand.

"I think if I cut this branch off it'll fit." I remained silent. Dan talks to himself when working on any project, large or small. He expects no conversational input and is oblivious to any that may be offered.

The lower branch fell away. The tree once again failed to fit into the stand. I heard a mumbled expletive but chose to ignore the curse. A little less gently Dan put the tree down again and surveyed the situation. I watched as he took hold of yet another lower branch and tugged.

"I'll have to cut this one too," he muttered. I felt a laugh gurgling up, but bit the sides of my mouth to stop the progression. The situation did not call for unsolicited input.

Dan took the saw and cut through the offending branch. It fell to the sheet. The once lush, thick pine appeared sparse. It was going to need extra tinsel in order to look full again. This thought I kept to myself. My suppressed laugh, however, came up unbidden. I disguised it with a cough. Another expletive came out loud and clear. By now, Dan was in a death battle with the pine tree. It was man against the wild.

"Okay," he said. "This is the one that needs to go." Saw in hand once more, he cut into a larger protrusion on the side of the trunk. Back and forth the saw cut into the offending spot. Finished, he drew the saw away and half of the remaining tree fell with a thud to the floor. What remained of the once regal tree was too emaciated to hold lights or tinsel but did fit nicely into the stand. There was no mistaking my laughter this time.

Dan, failing to see the humor, threw what was left of the tree out onto the front lawn. Without a word to me, he drove back to the lot and purchased another tree. It was a beautiful tree that fit into the stand on the first attempt. We did not speak of the tree trimming incident again.

By some standards, our evenings appeared mundane and boring. Following dinner, I cleaned our tiny kitchen to perfection, making it spotless and orderly. Dan sat in front of our fourteen-inch black and white television that set on a cheap metal cart with wheels, making it convenient to move to a different spot or even into another room. That was superfluous as our entire house was 700 square feet. It was possible to view the television screen from almost anywhere in the house.

As certain as the sun rising and setting each day, our television was tuned to *Gunsmoke*, starring James Arness, on Monday nights.

On Tuesday nights we watched *Combat,* starring Vic Morrow. Dan sat in our only living room chair, black rimmed glasses sliding down his nose, to await his two never-to-be-missed television shows. If we were invited to play cards or table games with another couple on one of the sacrosanct nights, then we would arrive after Matt Dillon had dealt with the last evil cowboy, sat for a drink with Miss Kitty and said good night to Chester. If Tuesday brought an invitation, then not until Vic Morrow had ordered his men to move forward, engage the enemy for a battle or two, gathered up the wounded and sat to smoke his last cigarette, did we venture forth.

I happily lived each day according to some obscure script.

From the onset, we became two people sharing a house and a bed, but not our lives. And from the moment we stepped across the threshold into married life, the gulf began to widen. I remained reticent to speak independently, fearing scorn. The lies told to me my entire life morphed into a bizarre reality. Danny, the acknowledged master and accountable to no one, began to pick up where, for a brief honeymoon period, he had left off. His life mutated into what he saw growing up. He carried on as a single man. My blinders firmly in place, I went about my solitary life. Now married, we became the perfect storm.

CHAPTER SIX

———∞∞∞———

When God puts us in the furnace, His hand is on the
thermostat and His eye is on the clock.

Rev. Andy Lapin

July of 1967 changed our lives forever. Since my parents' divorce in 1965, my mother had faded into and out of several less than idyllic relationships. In 1966 she met Stan, a generous, caring man who swept her up. They fell deeply in love and married. My mother was laughing again, happy and full of life. Danny and I attended the garden wedding at her Lincoln Park home, a suburb of Detroit. I was six months pregnant at the time.

Just ten days following the joyous occasion, Stan died suddenly of a heart attack. There had been no warning. My mother was now a widow. The momentary taste of happiness was ripped away; leaving her alone again. It seemed cruel that she should have joy within her grasp for those brief moments only to watch it disappear.

Months passed, time I have little recollection of as sharing with my mother. Long ago, I had put her on the outside of my world and now married, that had not changed. All my energy, my loyalty, and my attentions were focused on my new life. As in my teen years, my mother had no place in my life. That decision was entirely mine. It was a decision that I would not come to fully understand until later in my life.

My mother met someone new. They became engaged. She was happy once again, perhaps believing that surely fate would not again stomp its steel-toed boot on her face. She and her fiancé, Art Zimmerman, were married quietly in a private ceremony. They went on a honeymoon, a ten day trip traveling throughout Indiana and Illinois.

Michael, just nine years old and the youngest of my siblings, lived with my mother in Lincoln Park. He came to stay with Danny and me while the bride and groom were away. Julie was just four months old. Michael was quiet and timid. Julie responded to Michael's smiles and playful gestures. Our lives felt routine, even normal, not the pre-curser to the merciless, virulent storm approaching our young lives.

Michael had been with us just a few short days. We were in bed, the house quiet, and Danny and I had drifted into sleep. At 2 a.m. the telephone rang. Our only telephone set on a stand in the small living room. I awoke and stumbled, half asleep, to answer the ringing before either Julie or Michael were awakened.

"Hello," I said. I stood holding the receiver to my ear, eyes still shut with sleep, shielding them from the glare of the table lamp I had turned on as I tripped my way to the telephone.

"Mom's dead." My brother, Nick's, two words shot like bullets from a gun.

"What?" I was awake now. "How? When?" I croaked the words into the mouthpiece. A strange, surreal stillness settled over me.

"A car accident," he said just as abruptly as he had uttered his first words.

"Oh," my voice trailed off. "Okay."

We hung up. I was numb. It did not seem real. It was the middle of the night. I was just sleeping in bed with my husband. My small daughter was asleep in her crib. My brother Michael was asleep on a bed in the same room. That was real. This could not be. I stared

36

at the telephone. I went back to the bedroom and crawled back into bed beside my husband.

"Who was it?" Danny asked, half asleep.

"My brother, Nick," I said. I silently pulled the covers up over me and did not speak. I did not want to say the words aloud.

"Well, what did he want at this time of night," Danny said more as a statement than a question.

"My mother's dead," I said. The words had little meaning. Dead. What does that mean? I could not grab ahold of the thing that would make the words real.

"What?" Danny, fully awake now, shot up in bed to look down at me. "How? Where? When?" The force of his words made me look up into his face as the truth began to set in.

"I don't know," I said.

Danny got out of bed and went to the telephone. He dialed my brother's number. They talked for several minutes. I was only feet away in the small house but heard nothing of the conversation. Just as I had been able to do all my life, I detached from the ugliness wrapping itself around me.

The rest of the night passed. Predictably, Julie was the first one awake. Danny and I went through the routines of a Saturday morning. Neither of us spoke of this ugly thing gnarling its way into our lives. Michael did not yet know. By mid-morning Julie was down for a nap and Michael had gone outdoors to play.

"I can't tell him," I was crying for the first time since the telephone call in the middle of the night. "I can't do it." Dan and I stood together in our small living room. There were so many things to do, telephone calls to make, but nothing could go forward until Michael was told.

"I'll talk to him," Danny's voice was low. He went out the backdoor and called to Michael to join him on the porch. They sat huddled together and Dan put his arm around Michael's shoulders.

My place ought to have been there, sitting with both of them, while my baby brother had his heart sliced in two. Instead, I stayed in the confines of the house, near the door, but out of reach. Once again, life was out of control. My universe, the one I had so carefully planned and worked to make happen, was falling to pieces. This was not supposed to happen. My life was ordered and had boundaries for the first time. Every ounce of energy I possessed was spent in guarding the perimeters of this life. Now it was cracking, shattering and falling down around me. A panic I had not felt for a long time reared its ugly head. I was losing the gossamer thread of control so delicately wrapped around my pretend universe.

I could not hear the words but saw Michael's shoulders shake, his head dropped to his chest and the sobs began. They were not loud but deep and wrenching. I cried too. Dan cried. They sat together a long time.

That morning on the porch steps as he cried, he looked at my husband and said, "What's going to happen to me?"

Dan's immediate response, "You're going to live with us."

And he did. Despite our immaturity, our lack of parenting skills, the idiotic mistakes we made along the way, Michael grew to be a wise, loving, intelligent, successful man. We made many mistakes in his upbringing but we loved him. We were a family. Not perfect, but an intact family. So much so that when Julie was eight years old, she came to me with a question.

Running in from outdoors playing with friends, Julie stopped me as I was cooking and said, "Mom is Michael my brother or my uncle?"

Taken aback, it occurred to me that we had never made the distinction. It had just never come up and we did not think of it. I replied, "Well actually, he's your uncle."

"Oh," she said and went back outdoors to her friends.

That was all there was to it. Brother or uncle, it did not matter to Julie. He was Michael and she loved him.

Later, and alone, Danny and I talked about what needed to be done next. Shirley Ann, just fifteen years old, lived with Milly. She too, had stayed after the death of our father. My sister needed to be told. Danny called his mother with the news so she might tell Shirley Ann. Hearing of death over the telephone was, as we had recently experienced, like a knife being thrust through your chest. Once again, I left the task to someone else. Now, forty years later, I realize I was a child myself, ill-equipped to deal with such a devastating tragedy. But then, in my mind, I was running.

After the call from Danny, Milly went to Shirley Ann and said that they, along with Teresa would need to drive downstate.

"Your mother's been in a car accident," she said and walked out of Shirley's bedroom.

Later in the day as they packed to leave for the long drive to Madison Heights where we lived, Milly said casually, "You'll need a dress for the funeral." Shirley Ann began crying, then sobbing.

Teresa said to her mother, "Mom, she didn't know she was dead."

It was cruel and thoughtless, but typical of the woman speaking the words. In the short time following my father's death, Milly had withdrawn what pseudo-affection or attention she had so meagerly and insincerely meted out to me and my sister. I was experiencing it more subtly because I was, after all, her daughter-in-law. Milly's change toward me was quiet stealth and purposeful. Her thought-less treatment of my sister that day was not unusual; but, even for her, it was brutal.

The funeral was crowded with people, most of whom I did not know. I recall only snippets and brief snapshots of the day. People crying. The casket, my mother's face, her hands folded, a Rosary wrapped between her long, slender fingers. My mother had beauti-ful, feminine hands. She kept her fingernails manicured, painting her long nails red to accentuate their womanly appearance.

My mother was buried in St. Clair, Michigan, a small city on Lake St. Clair. We drove to the cemetery. My mother's grave was far up and in a corner of the vast cemetery. Other family graves, Schneiders and Zelkes, were in close proximity to one another but far from my mother's. Shirley Schneider-Wener lay in a far off cor-ner, next to where two drives converged into the cemetery.

When my mother died, more than her physical body passed to a place I could not go. Gone forever was the only person with whom I shared a unique bond. She had carried me in her womb and nurtured me by her own life's blood. I would never again have the opportunity to bridge the awful gap, the ugly chasm that had encompassed us during, after and since my parent's divorce, and since that black time when I had left to follow my father and his mistress. Forever silenced were words of comfort and understanding that we might have shared. I would never be allowed the opportunity to look back with maturity and wisdom of my own to find the words to beg her forgiveness for my selfish acts. An irrevocable edict had gone out to declare *The End* to any future in which my arms could hold on to a mother and she to me. A new seal was placed upon my lips so that I could never say *I love you mom*. My ears echoed empty sounds regardless of how desperately I wanted to hear *I love you Christine*, from the only woman I could or would ever call *mother*.

A future died for my mother. She would never cherish grandchildren, brag to her friends of how smart and talented are her grandchildren, or be called *Grandma* by excited voices. But a future died for me as well. If I had felt alone in the world when my father died, I felt sealed in a room of regrets and lost possibilities when my mother died. Never before, nor since, have I so profoundly felt a loss. I heard the sound of an iron gate as it shut and sealed off a future I was unable to even imagine. I was incapable of mourning for what I was equally incapable of imagining or ever hope to regain. You cannot repeat having a mother in your life.

When my mother lost her life at just forty-three years old, an entire lifetime of memories were lost; vanished at first in grief and then sorrow. My brief past of nineteen years, with a mere fifteen of them living with my mother, faded until they were non-existent, swallowed up and then evaporated. The memories of family, of tradition and sentiment are kept alive by the telling and re-telling, passed down from mother to daughter. Gone forever were my opportunities to tell and re-tell stories of my mother and me. She would never relate to me my first day of school or a special shopping trip for just the two of us. We would never laugh together over my first crush at six years old. I would never ask her to relate to me what I was like as a baby and did she see the same things in my own daughter. Even more tragically perhaps are the future and possible memories I would never experience. I would never recall telephone conversations with my mother about her grandchildren, relating funny things my children had done or said. I would never hear her laugh and tell me how alike my children are to me. Gone forever were any hopes of calling my mother, crying to ask her advice and hearing wisdom and comfort in her voice if not her words. Gone was the possibility of ever, for the rest of my life, hearing someone call me *daughter* and to say she loves me. I was never again to have the privilege of calling this special woman *mom*. Gone was the opportunity to say *I love you mom* to the only woman so deserving of those words.

A past and a future lie buried in a corner grave in St Clair, Michigan. Something important and vital to me as a woman evaporated the day Shirley Marie Wener died. I did not recognize it then but the results and ensuing consequences would continue to rise up over the years. As desperately as I have tried in the years since her death to claw my way to a memory, however brief and faint, there are none.

I am both angry and desolate that I cannot.

CHAPTER SEVEN

I have many regrets, and I'm sure everyone does. The stupid things you do, you regret, if you have any sense, and if you don't regret them, maybe you're stupid.

Katherine Hepburn

I would argue that at eighteen and twenty-three years old, you are ill-equipped, if not incapable, of making life long decisions. But, that is precisely what we had done. We married and now had a child. Dan and I grew up in homes where lies and deceit were the norm, affection and recognition meted out sparingly, if not conditionally, and honest communication became the proverbial dead elephant in the middle of the room. We carried our well learned traits over into our new lives.

One of the few topics that Danny and I discussed before we married was that I would be a stay-at-home mom. We both believed strongly that it was important for our children to live in a stable environment. Paramount to that stability was creating a home where mom was present. Equally, Danny believed as strongly that as a man and father, he was responsible for providing whatever it took to make it all possible. It was a time when the voices of criticism and disdain for stay-at-home moms were yet hushed whispers.

Julie was walking by the time she was ten months old. And, as does every parent, we were convinced that our daughter far exceeded all other babies born from time's beginning until and through eternity. Julie soon went from her walker, a metal contraption with a cloth seat, to toddling. She freely roamed from room to room, never out of sight because every room was visible from the living room. The bathroom door remained closed. I was not concerned with possible germs in the bathroom because I kept it bleach sterile clean. But I was afraid she would drown in the toilet bowl. Perhaps far-fetched but as a new parent I was prepared for every contingency.

The front entrance to our house was a standard wooden door with a small window at the top for viewing. Facing the heavy wooden door was an aluminum door with two parts; the top, approximately four foot in height, and the bottom portion, about two foot in height, all surrounded by lightweight aluminum. The top and bottom portions were glass. In the summer the glass was replaced by screen. The handle of the aluminum door had a slip lock on it. The lock worked more as a way to keep the door from accidentally opening than a deterrent to keep someone out. We kept the inner wooden door open, allowing light into the small living room, but made certain to latch the small lock on the aluminum door. Julie enjoyed standing at the door, pounding on the glass with her tiny fists and watching the activities outside.

It was October and sunny. The temperatures rose into the high 60s with an easy breeze and no clouds. Julie and I were home alone. We had just come back into the house from the backyard and taking freshly laundered diapers off the clothesline. The house was quiet. I sat on the couch folding the clean diapers from my wicker laundry basket. Julie helped me by dragging the diapers out of the basket and littering them throughout the house.

Our mailbox was attached to the house just outside the front door. The familiar clunk of the mailbox lid alerted me that our mailman had deposited the day's mail. Retrieving the mail did not require leaving the house, just leaning out the door to reach into the box. As I did so, a piece of mail fell to the ground to the side of the porch. Without thinking, I jumped down to retrieve the envelope. As soon as my feet hit the soft ground, the door swung shut and I heard the familiar 'click' of the lock.

I stepped back onto the porch, grabbed the handle and pulled. Nothing. I shook the handle. Nothing. I rattled the door. Nothing. I was locked outside and Julie was inside, alone and walking around. I knew the back door was locked. It remained locked whenever Danny was not home. He reminded me each day to keep it locked.

Julie waddled over to the door. "Hi sweetie," I said. She smiled. "Open the door for mommy, honey." I pointed to the door handle and smiled at her encouragingly.

My request was made out of desperation because Julie could not reach the handle. I began to panic. My ten month old daughter was walking around inside and I was outside. I looked around to find something that would get me back inside the house, but kept my eyes on Julie. I could not leave the door to walk to a neighbor for help because I wanted to keep Julie in sight. Talking and cooing to keep her attention was only temporary. She had the attention span of a ten month old. Julie quickly toddled off to places I could not see. I called to her. She ignored me.

I thought of a solution. Admittedly it was not one of my more stellar moments, but in my own defense it was the only one that seemed logical to me at the time and in the circumstances.

Julie came back to the door to watch mommy make funny faces. Quickly losing interest once again, Julie walked away from the door. As soon as I saw her a safe distance from the door, I stood back on one foot and kicked my other foot through the bottom glass of the door. The glass shattered and fell into the house but did not fly far from the front of the door.

Unfortunately, one piece of jagged glass remained inside the aluminum frame. As I kicked, I stumbled backwards and my ankle came down onto the point of the glass. I hopped back and saw a shard of glass projecting from the side of my foot, blood spewing from the hole. My white sock turned red and my shoe was fast filling up with blood. I forced my eyes away from the bloody mess. Instead I reached inside the door, unlocked it and slumped down just inside the door. The sound of the breaking glass got Julie's attention. She ran to me as fast as her short, chubby legs would carry her. I grabbed her up in my arms and held tight.

The telephone set on a small end table next to the couch. I inched myself over to the telephone, holding Julie and trying to ignore the blood trail following me. I telephoned Pat, my next-door neighbor.

"Pat, I've hurt myself," I said. "Can you come over and get Julie?"

The line went dead. I strained to reach over to put the receiver back onto its cradle and still keep ahold of Julie. Before I could let go of the telephone receiver, Pat was at my door.

"What happened?" She stared at the shattered glass and the blood that was, by this time, forming a large pool around my foot. Without waiting for an answer, she took Julie from my arms, leaned out the door and shouted to another neighbor. "Mary, get over here, now!"

Mary appeared almost immediately. Between the two, it was decided I must go to the emergency room. Someone called for emergency help. The ensuing chaos resembled a sort of bizarre crime scene; me on the floor sitting amid broken glass, a pool of blood settled under my foot, and a trail of blood leading to the porch. Pat held Julie while Mary picked up glass. Pat grabbed towels from the kitchen.

"Here," Pat said, "Use these to mop up some of that blood." She handed the towels to Mary. "We better use one to wrap that foot."

Together they wrapped my bleeding foot being careful not to dislodge the glass protruding from the skin. By this time, my tiny front yard was crowded with neighbors. The Police came. A fire truck came roaring up in front of the house. An ambulance showed up. Explaining this to Danny was going to be a challenge.

The fire truck left. The ambulance left when it was decided that the Police would take me to the emergency room. Another neighbor was assigned to bring me back home. Once in the emergency room, doctors found the cut to be deeper and larger than at first thought. The wound was cleaned and stitched back together. I went home with orders from the doctor to stay off my feet and keep my foot elevated. I thought that was funny but did not say so. I had a ten month old.

Michael was home from school by the time we returned entertaining Julie. Within a very short time, a golf ball sized pocket of blood formed around the wound, straining the stitches. Back to the emergency room. I was unstitched, cleaned up again, restitched and sent back home with a reminder to stay off my feet. Yes, I remember that instruction.

Pat and Mary stayed with me and finished cleaning the bloody mess. Predictably, at 5:00 o'clock Danny came home from work.

"What happened," he asked, eyeing the empty spot where glass had been when he left that morning. Pat and Mary began explaining, both talking at once.

"You did what?" Danny shook his head and walked away. I remained convinced that my decision had been the correct course of action given the circumstances. But next time, I might look for a brick to fling instead of my foot.

Danny's logical focus kept us grounded most of the time, but, he too, had his moments as a parent that are probably best forgotten. He reveled in teaching his above average, super-intelligent daughter new things. On one particular occasion, he proudly announced to me that he had taught Julie, then just 15 months old, how to unscrew caps and lids.

"You did what? You shouldn't have done that," I said. "She could get into things that are dangerous."

"Oh, stop it," Danny said. "You worry too much. She'll be fine."

I was not convinced and within a few short days, my concern proved to be justified. Julie used her new skill to unscrew the top of a small bottle of cologne. She drank the entire bottle. That was my first call to the poison control center.

"Cheap cologne is mostly alcohol," the man on the line said, "so she'll be fine."

It was a good thing I could only afford cheap cologne.

Not long after guzzling a bottle of cologne, Julie found Michael's model airplane kit. Once again, using her new skill proudly taught by her dad, she unscrewed the cap on the airplane glue and sucked a portion of the nasty stuff down. My second call to poison control.

Weeks passed and I was confident I had a handle on the cap unscrewing issue when Danny struck again.

"Hey, Chris," he called. "Come out here." He and Julie were in the backyard playing. Danny's patience with his daughter was limitless. He spent hours with her doing whatever he saw that made her happy.

I stepped out onto the porch. Julie, now eighteen months old, stood near the gate of our chain link fence.

"Watch this," he grinned at me. He set Julie in front of the gate and said, "Go ahead sweetie, show mommy what you can do."

Julie put her tiny feet, clad in white high-tops, in the links of the fence gate. I gaped in horror as her little, pudgy legs crawled, one link at a time, all the way to the top of the gate. Danny smiled a proud father smile.

"Are you insane?" I put my head in my hands to keep from seeing Julie fall backwards to the ground. She did not fall. Danny helped her down. He looked at her and gave her a kiss. Turning back to me, he shook his head and gave me the now familiar superior look.

"She can now get out of the yard at will." I was furious.

"Oh, she won't do that," he said. "You worry too much."

I walked back into the house muttering, "It's a good thing one of us does."

Years later as Julie grew and approached the inevitable conclusion that Santa Claus was not the person she thought he was, she came to her Dad for confirmation.

"Daddy, I don't think Santa Claus is real." Dan sat on the edge of Julie's bed, giving her a goodnight kiss.

"Honey, why do you say that?" He proceeded cautiously.

"Because, when I opened my new pajamas from Santa, the tag said, JCPenney," she said.

Rather than force an explanation, Dan decided it was time to come clean. "Sweetheart, you're right," he began. "Mom and I give you the presents because we love you and it's fun for us to see you so excited."

"I thought so." Julie did not appear devastated by the news. Had Dan stopped there, Julie would have kissed her dad and fallen asleep, comfortable with the news about Santa.

"You know honey," he went on, "Santa is fun to believe in when you are young. It makes Christmas exciting. It's the same with the Easter Bunny. . ."

I heard a wail from the upstairs. "Oh no!" Julie cried, "Not the Easter Bunny! I didn't know about the Easter Bunny!"

After several minutes of consoling Julie and wiping her tears, Dan came down the stairs. I stared at him. He shrugged sheepishly, "I thought she already knew about the Easter Bunny."

CHAPTER EIGHT

———⊶⊷———

God's efforts are strongest when our efforts are useless.

Max Lucado

For as long as I can remember my dream was to have a large family. Once the identity of my future husband was a *fait accompli* I concentrated on the children we would produce; hair color, eye color and of course gender. Our first would be a boy; I was sure, with big brown eyes like Danny's, dark brown curly hair, again like Danny's. It simply did not enter my realm of thinking that a redhaired, green-eyed baby girl would make the first appearance. But she had. When Julie was not yet one year old, we talked about having a second child. It was easy enough the first time

After six months of trying to become pregnant and not succeeding, I sought out a physician for what I hoped would be simple answers and a quick remedy.

"The first thing we are going to do is to have you keep a calendar of your cycle," the doctor told me.

"What does that mean?"

"Every month when a woman ovulates, her body temperature will rise just a bit," he explained. "By keeping track of your

51

temperature every day for a month or two, it will indicate if and when you are ovulating."

The doctor handed me a packet of information along with several sheets of calendar days. Along one side of each sheet were temperature points. By tracking each day's body temperature, the sheet became a graph showing the rise and fall of my cycle.

"It's important that you take your temperature every morning, *before* you get out of bed," he emphasized *before*. "Don't move more than necessary."

"Okay," I said. It seemed simple enough and I was certain that in a month or two I would be pregnant.

"One more thing," the doctor said as I turned to leave. "Mark with a circle each time you and your husband have intercourse."

That was a new point.

The next morning, the chart, an ink pen and thermometer set on the nightstand next to where I slept. Each morning thereafter the thermometer was in my mouth, under my tongue while I lay as still as possible for three minutes. This ritual was performed for thirty days. Each degree on the chart clearly indicated, with circles marked as well. At the end of one month, I went back to the doctor, chart in hand.

Looking at my handiwork, the doctor laughed, "Well, there are certainly a lot of circles."

As embarrassing as that remark was, making me uncomfortable, I was to learn over the next ten years, nothing about infertility was private or personal.

"You don't seem to be ovulating," he said. "Let's give it one more month to see if this was an anomaly."

When another month showed no spike on my chart indicating ovulation, the doctor suggested a series of hormone shots to jump start my ovaries into spitting out an egg or two. The shots worked, or so it seemed, by the clear spikes on my most recent chart. But after three more months of not becoming pregnant, I was back in the doctor's office.

"I think we need to check your husband's sperm count," he mused as he checked my newest charts. "This clearly shows ovulation."

"Okay," I said slowly. "How is that done?"

He explained in detail and handed me a small, sterile cup with a lid.

"Really?" I said. "And what do we do with it then?" This was not sounding good. I imagined myself explaining the procedure to Danny. The doctor's next instructions captured my full attention.

"It's important to keep the specimen warm," he said. "Sperm will only survive about twenty minutes out of the body."

"Really?"

"So within twenty minutes, get it here to my office," he cautioned.

"Okay." The one word came out more a question than a reply of understanding.

"And keep it warm," he reminded me.

On the short drive home, I practiced explaining the delicate procedure to Danny. I was young and not the sophisticated woman I pretended. My face flushed hot with embarrassment as I envisioned the scene.

"So, here's what the doctor wants you to do." I said the words aloud in the car and groaned. The little sterile plastic cup set beside me, sealed in an equally sterile plastic bag.

In retrospect, of the numerous medical procedures I experienced during the years of infertility, the little plastic sterile cup was a blimp on the massive screen of the embarrassing and painful.

Twenty-four hours later I stood at the front desk of the doctor's office. Tucked inside my bra, the warmest spot on my body was the small plastic cup of my husband's sperm.

I leaned in close to the receptionist, "I was told to bring this to the office and to tell you it is immediate." I slowly reached inside my bra and brought out the tiny cup and handed it over the counter to the receptionist.

"What is it?" She took it and stared at the contents.

My face burned hot. I longed to make a hasty retreat. "It's a sample for a sperm analysis," I kept my voice as low as possible.

"For what?" Obviously she had no problems raising her voice and my whispers failed to indicate to her that this was a private issue.

"Sperm analysis." I whispered.

She took the cup from my hand, turned to look over her shoulder and shouted, "I have a specimen for sperm analysis. Somebody want to get it ASAP?"

The entire waiting room heard her and turned to look at me. Stupid woman, I thought to myself. The receptionist took my name and made note of my chart number. I made my hasty retreat. Still new to the world of infertility and its treatments, I was embarrassed that my private life was open to public eye. That actuality was soon swallowed up as I became simply a uterus with ovaries and fallopian tubes.

"The good news," the doctor said on my next visit, "is your husband has some strong sperm, lots of swimmers in there."

"That's great," I said. "Then why am I not pregnant"

"Well," he said, "there could be a variety of causes."

"Such as?" I asked. Not having a large family was not a part of my perfect life. The more questions I asked, the fewer the answers. In 1967 medicine, no one had answers. Instead, the doctors kept throwing things at the wall, hoping something would stick.

My plans remained focused, and this part included another baby. Danny was neither disappointed nor upset. He listened as I related to him the rounds of tests, my sadness each month at not being pregnant, and willingly enough, cooperated with each new idea the doctor presented. He listened but did not become engaged. He went through the motions as he would for any job that needed his immediate attention. As his wife, I was just that, a job, apportioned a specific amount of time, material and attention, just enough to keep me quiet and not disturbing his life outside of our marriage.

Pursuing infertility was all consuming. It was frustrating and painful to realize that my life was not my own. I could not, as much as I willed it, make my body do what it was supposed to do naturally. Life became a see-saw, up and down, from hope to despair, month after month. As the days and weeks passed, I burrowed deeper inside myself, determined to fix whatever was preventing me from becoming pregnant. My focus, which was morphing into obsession, had the unfortunate effect of fixing blinders on my eyes, aiding me in ignoring what was going on around me.

Danny was increasingly withdrawn from our lives. He crossed into coming and going according to a private darkness that became an abyss. He grew moody and silent. Deciding that I must be the cause of his unhappiness, I dared not question anything he did or said, fearing that my actions would only drive him farther away and into an even darker place. I survived by detaching from anything that tasted of conflict. To assert myself was unthinkable to the point of making me physically ill. Total acquiescence was my mantra.

CHAPTER NINE

———— ⌘ ————

No word exists in the Hebrew language for coincidence.
Rabbi Daniel Lapin

After four years as an apprentice, working for E.W. Evans under sheet metal journeymen employed there, Dan's schooling was completed. He was now officially a card-carrying sheet metal journeyman. Along with the status, his pay became commensurate with a full-fledged union member. We enjoyed all the accompanying benefits as well; vacation pay, full coverage medical insurance, and sick pay. It was a substantial increase in his pay checks, prompting us to begin planning for things we had put off until finances allowed.

Our first large purchase was a vehicle. After selling the Bonneville, we acquired a 1964 Ford Fairlane, boring blue in color, standard transmission and four doors, also boring. It is said that automobiles make a statement about the owner's lifestyle. If that is so, then our latest acquisition spoke loud and clear: boring, unexciting and slow moving. But it was reliable, had no body damage or rust and was paid-for-in-full. Dan decided it was time for a new, sporty model car to match his status as he saw himself;

successful and going places. I thought nothing of a particular make or model. It would be nice to have a new car was the extent of my yearning.

After researching makes and models, going from dealer to dealer and test driving various vehicles, he decided on a Pontiac LeMans. It was the first brand new car Dan had owned and every detail was meticulously thought out, leaving nothing to chance or anyone else's decision. He opted for silver exterior, red leather interior, bucket seats, rally wheels, AM FM radio and automatic transmission. This car was top of the line. We were on the move upward.

The faithful, albeit boring, blue Fairlane was sold. We were not so far moved up in status that we could afford two vehicles. There was no reason to own two cars. I was a stay-at-home mom, living in a small neighborhood with no plans to go anywhere on my own. On the rare occasions when I required the use of our one vehicle I packed Julie and Michael into the car and drove Danny to work at Evans and Company on Nine Mile Road and Woodward Avenue, returning at day's end to pick him up. The drive was minimal and took just fifteen minutes from our driveway. Once Dan showed me the route to and from the shop, I robotically drove it the same way, never varying for fear of getting hopelessly lost. It was not unusual to see other wives doing the same thing on many mornings. A two-car family was not yet the norm and was most certainly seen as a luxury. We purchased our new car in March.

Some months earlier, I explained to Dan that I would need the car for the day. "Julie has a well-baby check-up at the pediatrician," I said. "Let me drive you to work, then come back to pick you up." It was our usual routine whenever I had appointments.

"We're meeting Ron and Marilyn after work at their house for a BBQ, remember?" I had forgotten the plans and said so. "Okay, I'll drive home with Ron and you and Julie can meet me at their house after work," he said.

The plan sounded logical. As I drove Dan to work, he gave me detailed directions to Ron and Marilyn's house. "Do you think you can do it without getting lost?"

The humor in his voice did not escape me. I did not find it amusing. "Yes, I can find my way," I replied, using the same back-handed humor. "I'm not an idiot." The rest of our ride was in silence.

The directions were straight forward and precise. The route was a major highway to another highway, a couple of turns into their neighborhood and I would arrive. It looked and sounded easy. That was the plan.

At four o'clock I loaded Julie and her diaper bag into the Fairlane, headed out of our small neighborhood, turned onto John R and began my journey. Dan's written directions set on the seat next to me. Julie, dressed in a pretty pink dress and white bonnet, sat in her car seat beside me. We drove for what seemed a long time, much longer than I had anticipated. Traffic was heavy this time of day, I reasoned, so it only seemed to take forever.

"Where am I?" I said the words out loud. "Oh no, I'm lost." I was frantically looking for street signs. "This can't be happening. It was so straight forward when I looked at the directions." Julie looked at me, smiled, and pulled on her pacifier.

I pulled into a car dealership, got Julie out of her car seat and we went inside to the business offices. A smiling salesman appeared and walked over to me, "Hi. Can I help you?"

I smiled back. "Yes, do you have a telephone I can use?" I did not mention that I was hopelessly lost. So lost in fact, I was unsure if I was even going in the right direction to anywhere.

"Yes, certainly. Follow me." In his office, he offered me a chair and put a black rotary telephone in front of me. Holding Julie in one arm, I dialed Ron and Marilyn's number from memory. Marilyn answered.

"Hi Marilyn. Is Dan there? Can I talk to him?" I waited. Dan came on the line. "I'm lost." I heard him laugh but did not chuckle in return. By this time I was hot, tired and Julie was getting hungry.

"Where are you?" He asked.

"I have no idea." My reply was short and I offered nothing further by way of explanation.

"Well, where are you calling *from*?" He emphasized the last word.

"A Ford dealer."

"A Ford dealer *where?*"

"I don't know." This time my words came out quiet and clipped.

"Ask somebody," he said, equally terse.

I turned to the smiling salesman and said, "Where am I?" I was certain I saw a surprised look, but, he hesitated only a heartbeat before replying. I repeated the location to Dan.

"What?" He shouted the words into the telephone. "How did you get way over there?"

"I don't know," I spat out the words. "I don't even know where I am so how can I tell you how I got here?"

"Okay, okay," he sensed I was on the edge. "Here's how to get *here* from *there*," he began. I stopped him.

"No," I said. "I'm staying right here. You come and get me."

As Julie and I sat in the dealership waiting to be retrieved, I wondered how and why these things always happen to me. I was not happy.

May marked our three year anniversary. Although Dan occasionally went out in the evening alone or to meet friends, we rarely ventured out as a couple. Still, I wanted to mark the day with a celebration. I telephoned Dan's sister. Janet, three years Dan's junior, married with two small children, lived with her husband, Ron, in Berkley.

"Janet, can I ask a favor?"

"Sure, what do you need?" Janet asked.

"Our anniversary is this coming Tuesday," I explained. "And I want to surprise Danny."

"Okay," she said, "What can I do?"

"I'd like to bring the kids over in the afternoon, and then pick them up later in the evening," I said.

"Are you and Dan going someplace special?" Janet asked.

"No, I'm going to cook us a nice meal right here so we can be alone."

"That does sound romantic," she said. "What time do you want to bring the kids over?" We agreed on a time and I hung up.

On Tuesday I drove Dan to work and spent the better part of the day shopping and preparing the food, the house, and myself. After driving the kids to Janet's house in Berkley, another memo-rized-no-detours- route, I made a last stop at the grocery store near our house.

The shopping center, located at 14 Mile Road and John R, one half mile from our house, consisted of Kresge's Dimestore, Hudson's Department Store and one grocery store. The large park-ing lot was spacious and in the afternoon almost empty, affording ample parking spaces. Dan's 1969 silver, sporty LeMans with the rally wheels was a mere three months old. I was extra cautious and chose a spot far removed from the scant number of vehicles already parked in the concrete lot. One lone grocery cart set adja-cent to my car. I immediately took hold and wheeled it into the store with me, imagining a rogue gust of wind pushing its menac-ing steel into the pristine silver paint.

As I looked back at the car, I breathed a sigh of relief. A sudden unforeseen tragedy averted. The shiny, sporty vehicle set alone, far from possible sneak attacks.

The items on my list were few but I lingered in the grocery store. As a young wife, I relished the art of grocery shopping, going up and down the aisles, pausing to consider what and how many of the myriad items on display to put in my basket. The cornucopia of provisions available fascinated me then and still does today.

Once my dinner provisions were purchased, bagged, and put back into the grocery cart, I headed to the still alone and un-accosted shiny silver vehicle. The large brown grocery sacks loaded into the trunk, I settled comfortably and a little reverently into the driver's bucket seat. My thoughts were on getting home, preparing a romantic dinner, making myself glamorous and sexy, all before I left to pick up my husband. I smiled thinking of his surprise, and hopefully, delight at our upcoming evening.

The parking lot was expansive and still near deserted. Each allotted spot was divided by yellow lines and noted further by a concrete guard, ensuring and reminding drivers to stay within the allotted space. I was careful to note each one. The guards stood approximately three feet in height, twelve to eighteen inches in diameter and for extra measure were painted white, with bright red paint on the top third of the solid concrete. The very sight screamed CAUTION! WATCH FOR US!

I turned the key in the engine, the engine came to life and I shifted to reverse. Leaning my head slightly out the opened window, I noticed an object next to the rear panel of the car. Immediately on alert, I opened my door to peer more closely to determine what, if any, threat the object posed to the car. Leaning low, my head turned downward, the door slightly ajar; my foot rose off the brake and the car began a slow crawl in reverse.

THUD! My foot stomped immediately on the brake pedal, which prevented the driver's side door from being ripped off completely. In the almost imperceptible move back, the inside of the door came in full and abrupt contact with the guard post I had so carefully noted and avoided when I parked the car. Putting the car in park, my heart pounding, I studied the door for damage. It appeared unscathed. I marveled that I could be so lucky.

I pulled the door shut, intending to make a hasty getaway only to hear an unfamiliar and not pleasant clicking sound from the direction of the door. Although the door shut, it failed to line up correctly, making it appear off-center. It was drivable and so I drove home, imagining what a romance killer this was going to be.

Soon after unloading the groceries, trying unsuccessfully several times to get the door to shut and seal, I gave up and went inside. The telephone rang.

"Happy Anniversary!" Pam, my best friend since kindergarten, sang over the phone.

"Oh hi," I said, my mind still fumbling for a plausible explanation for the car door, one in which I did not appear an idiot. Nothing was coming to mind.

"What's wrong?" Pam heard my less than enthusiastic voice.

"Well, I'm not so sure how happy it's going to be now," I said.

"Why? What happened?" She asked. I explained the entire fiasco, berating myself for my blunder.

"It was an accident," Pam reminded me. Her voice oozed confidence. The seepage did not reach me.

"He's going to be so angry at me, Pam," I said.

"Then don't tell him," she said matter-of-factly.

"What?" I almost shouted. "He'll know it as soon as he sees the door, Pam. There's an obvious gap and the door won't shut all the way."

"Look," Pam explained, "tell him casually that you noticed the door won't shut. It's under warranty, right?"

"Yes, it's only three months old," I moaned. Danny's coveted car, and I did the first damage to it.

"Offer to take it in and have it looked at tomorrow," she said. "And then shut-up."

"Okay, I can try that. But if he asks me what happened, I can't lie to him." A panic was making itself comfortable inside my chest.

"Well, he may not ask."

That was true, I thought, and decided I had nothing to lose by trying Pam's suggestion. And if it worked, that would be very good.

Dan was surprised by our anniversary dinner and enjoyed the evening. My delight was dampened due to the silver monster in the driveway mocking me.

Later as we went out to the car to drive over to pick up the kids, I casually mentioned, "Oh, the driver's side door isn't shutting all the way."

"Really?" Dan said. He examined the door, testing it with numerous opening and closing attempts and finally agreed with me. The driver's side door did not shut properly.

Once at Janet's, Dan explained to Ron, her husband, the dilemma with the door. They studied the situation, closely examining the door, moving it back and forth, offering possible explanations but failing to arrive at a conclusion.

"Have Chris take it to the dealer tomorrow," Ron offered. "Let them figure it out."

"Yeah, that's a good idea," Dan agreed. Turning to me, he said, "You'll have to take me to work again tomorrow so you can get it to the dealership."

"Okay," I said. Except for that one word I remained mute on the mystery of the door.

The next day at the dealership, a mechanic studied the problem, examining the door much as Danny and Ron had done. Finally, he took the door off completely, made adjustments, put it back on and I drove away with the door fully restored.

No one ever asked me, "What happened".

CHAPTER TEN

———⊸⊛⊛⊖———

Everything reaps its own harvest; every act has its own reward
and before you covet the enjoyment, which another possesses,
you must first calculate the cost at which it was procured.

D.L. Moody

Over the ensuing months, our lives changed in quiet, subtle ways. Imperceptible things I was unable to define, but felt growing stronger every day, crept into our lives.

As a family we appeared the average couple with two children and a home in a blue-collar middle class neighborhood. Michael was in school and doing well. Julie was growing and getting enough hair for barrettes or ribbons. I was on monthly visits with my doctor still wondering why I failed to become pregnant. The small nagging inside my head began. *You can't get pregnant. Here is another failure of yours. What a disappointment you must be as a wife.*

My self-recriminations were reinforced as Dan continued to fade from my life. His dark moods and sullen disposition frightened me. Sudden anger, unlike Danny's usual happy disposition, erupted over the ridiculous. It seemed he looked for reasons to be angry, to allow what boiled inside an escape. Keeping to my firm patterns learned early on in life, I said nothing. His sudden bursts of anger kept me uneasy and silent. This behavior was to become a pattern repeated throughout our married lives. Too late I recognized the pattern for what it was. The ground beneath us was crumbling under the cacophony of lies and deceit, made more fertile by my fear and silence.

At twenty years old I was ill equipped to battle with such a vicious and ruthless enemy. I had entered the marriage innocent and unarmed. What I did not know then was an enemy, like a virulent flesh-eating bacteria, had entered my home. Our lives were slowly and quietly dying, if there had ever been life before. Still ignorant and fearful, I remained intent on becoming pregnant. I was sure that having another baby would bring us close once again. The truth was Danny and I had never been close. We were two people, living two lives.

Sitting at my now familiar spot in the doctor's office, he explained the next step to solving the mystery as to why I was not pregnant.

"We're going to do a post-coital test," he said.

I knew what coital meant and I knew what post meant. Putting them together did not sound good. "What does that involve?" I spoke the question, but dreaded the answer. As it turned out, I had good reason.

"We do a pelvic exam immediately following intercourse to determine if the sperm are active once deposited in the vagina," he said.

"So, I have sex with my husband and then come to your office?" Things cannot get worse, I thought to myself.

I was wrong.

"Right," he answered. "And remember sperm are active for only so long so you'll have to get here within twenty to thirty minutes following intercourse."

"Right." That part I remembered. He gave me instructions to come immediately to the desk and tell the receptionist I must be seen at once. I was remembering my last encounter with the receptionist.

I could hear it now. "Hey! This woman had sex less than twenty minutes ago. Somebody come and get the sperm!" My face grew hot.

66

Maybe she left. Or, she got fired.

The next day I stood at the desk quietly explaining to the same receptionist that I was to be seen immediately. The nurse must have briefed her before I arrived, because I was ushered quickly and quietly into an exam room.

"Hmmm." The doctor examined the specimen on the slide under a microscope. "Get dressed and we'll talk," he said as he left me alone to get dressed.

The nurse returned and ushered me into his private office.

"The sperm do not seem to be moving on the slide," he told me.

"What does that mean?" Discouragement blanketed over me. My heart pounded in my chest. This could not be good news.

"It could mean that for some unexplained reason, once inside your body your husband's sperm die." Hot tears welled up, clouding my vision. *It's my fault. I am to blame. It's my fault.* The tortuous refrain screamed inside my head, accusing me.

"But," he said, "We'll check one more time to be certain there are no other factors involved."

I left the office and once in my car, the tears came in a torrent of sadness and blame.

"What's wrong with me?" I sobbed. I sat alone in the parking lot and cried. Back home, I did not tell Danny what the doctor had said. He did not ask.

Days later, I was again in the office, feet up in stirrups, waiting for the verdict.

"Good news," my doctor said. "We've got strong, active swimmers." A weight lifted up off my chest and I let out the breath I had been holding. It was good news but little else. There was no epiphany to explain why I was not pregnant.

As the weeks passed I focused on one thing; getting pregnant. Danny showed little interest in my sadness and frustration. On the rare occasion when I attempted to talk about it and explain my feelings, I was dismissed with "quit worrying" or "just stop thinking about it."

His continued absences and dark moods convinced me the fault lay in me and my inability to have more children. I was the reason for his obvious unhappiness.

In reality, his focus was elsewhere, but close by, in our small neighborhood.

Doggedly, I pursued the next course of infertility treatments. The doctor appointments and testing gave me focus, a challenge. In what I believed to be a last ditch effort to find a cause, I was scheduled for a Hysterosalpingogram or HSG. Done in the hospital as an out-patient, the procedure required a general anesthetic. My doctor explained to Danny and me that a dye is inserted into the uterus, flows through the fallopian tubes indicating where or if there is a blockage preventing sperm and egg fertilization. That sounded hopeful. I was excited that perhaps the end was in sight. The thing, whatever it was, was about to be discovered and fixed.

The scheduled day arrived. I was given the anesthetic and taken into the operating room. Sometime later I awoke and saw Danny sitting next to my bed.

"Hi honey," Dan's voice was quiet. He kissed me.

"What did the doctor say?" My voice, still groggy from the anesthetic, was hoarse.

"He hasn't come in yet to tell us anything. They just brought you back to the room."

The doctor arrived a short time later.

"I'm sorry but we were unable to complete the test," he told us both. Tears sprang up into my eyes. I was angry and disappointed.

"Why not?" Dan asked.

"As the tube for the dye was inserted the uterus was punctured. A small puncture," he said. "But once that occurs, it's impossible to continue due to the risk of infection from contamination."

That was that. The test failure was more than just a disappointment. Later, what the test did not show was to nearly cost me my life.

Now twenty-one years old, I was married with a beautiful three year old daughter and trying my best to be a mom to my twelve year old brother. And feverishly working to prove myself a worthy wife.

You will never out think Satan. He can out think you all day long. But Satan cannot ever out think God.

Dan

STERLING HEIGHTS, MICHIGAN

1970 - 1975

CHAPTER ELEVEN

———⊶⊷———

There are many ways short of direct murder by which a man's life can be taken.

F.B. Meyer

Our brand new home was a three bedroom brick ranch-style located in the still growing neighborhood of Sterling Heights. Married just four years, we were ecstatic that purchasing a new home had gone from a possibility to a reality. The tiny house in Madison Heights sold in a hurried eight weeks. Friends helped us move our furniture from the 700 square feet of space on Barrington Street to the new 2000 square feet of living space on Idaho Drive. Our furniture, which had filled our smaller home, seemed miniature in the new space.

Michael, now fourteen years old, occupied one bedroom, a space all his own, not subject to Julie's search and seizure. Julie in a second bedroom, Dan and I occupied the third and biggest of the bedrooms. The spacious living area came with a mortgage increased by triple and corresponding house payments. For this, we spent considerable time weighing our options and calculating costs. It had been our practice since marrying that all financial decisions were made together. In this, we were equals. I also recognized that my husband possessed a sound business sense and I trusted, without question, that he had our family's best interest in mind. He was an excellent provider and money manager so if he said we could do this, then I knew it to be so.

The houses were newer and bigger, the lawns green and lined with shrubs and flowers but we were still a working class neighborhood. Dads left each morning to work and moms stayed home as homemakers. But there existed a chasm of differences between Barrington Street and Idaho Drive. My new neighbors did not troop from house to house every day and sit at kitchen tables drinking coffee and smoking cigarettes. The gossipy tales that flourished and fed the old neighborhood were silent on Idaho Drive. I knew little of my new neighbors. I liked it that way. Meeting new people intimidated me. Avoiding failure, or worse, someone not accepting me, chained me to an invisible wall. Living in a brick ranch house in a new subdivision did not change that.

At twenty-two years old, I continued to live with the Creature from the Black Lagoon chasing me, always swimming just under the surface of my life, waiting to grab me and pull me down into its menacing underworld. My life was paper and mirrors, pretending and following the motions. Since moving to Sterling Heights, I withdrew deeper into my Cinderella life. Living in a new neighborhood filled with new people, made it necessary to create the illusion once again.

Not surprisingly, it was not working any better than it had in Madison Heights. I was not Cinderella. Danny was not Prince Charming coming to rescue me. And there was no castle. My safely guarded universe was slipping. Danny and I quietly went about making our own lives separate and apart from each other. I did what I knew best how to do. I ignored anything that did not fit in with my created order. When a reality occasionally rose up to belch in my face, I burrowed deeper, telling myself new lies. Like a hamster on a wheel, I ran but got nowhere. A familiar pattern resurfaced. Danny was gone to unnamed places, doing unspecified tasks, absent from home and our lives. Danny, predictably, refused to answer my questions as to where he had been, why he had been gone, or with whom. As before, I was dismissed with a shrug and roll of his brown eyes. If pressed, he became angry. On the rare occasions, when I gathered the courage to push him or dared to accuse him of lying, his anger erupted and, predictably, I shut down. My own fear was enough to silence me.

As a child, I hid from my father's rage, cowering in corners, covering my head with a pillow to silence the screaming that came up to my bedroom, all in hopes it would just go away. Just as that little girl of long ago, I cowered, fleeing from truths that might slice into my make believe order.

Finally, out of desperation, I made an appointment with a counselor. One afternoon while I was gone from the house, the counselor called to confirm the appointment. Dan was home and took the call.

"Did you make an appointment with a counselor?" He asked. So much for client confidentiality.

"Yes," I said. My heart raced, afraid of his reaction. But it was surprising. Instead of becoming angry or demanding to know what was going on, he was charming and gentle.

"Why, honey?" he said as he knelt beside me. "What's wrong?" He took my hands in his. "Can I do anything? Why didn't you come and talk to me about what's bothering you?"

There it was. The soft words, affirmations of love and devotion, designed to keep me at bay and silent. At this point, I was like a well-trained pet that occasionally needed a reassuring pat on the head. And Dan, the slick snake oil salesman who knows the precise elixir for every ill, was all too ready to accommodate me.

"I know there's something wrong," I said quietly. "You don't come home after work and I know you're lying to me." The tears slid down my cheeks. My voice was low and trembling. Having truth on my side did nothing to bolster my fear of his reactions.

"Oh, honey, you know I love you," Danny said softly. "Do you love me?" He leaned close to my face, smiling his most genuine smile, white teeth flashing. The master manipulator, Danny knew what to say and how to say it, all designed to silence me. Once appeased and back in line, he returned to his own life.

"Of course I love you." Tears ran down my face and Danny put his arms around me. Satisfied that the danger of exposure was passed, he got up and walked away.

My life was a shadow operating with little substance. The voices inside me grew louder, calling me a coward one minute but warning me to keep quiet the next. The one sure way to quiet the voices was to go on with my pretend life, smiling and lying to myself. I saw myself as a cross between Pippy Longstockings and Snow White. On the one hand, I appeared bold, a little crazy even. I had answers for everyone and was not afraid to speak my mind. When I saw what I believed was an injustice, I was there on the spot to help defend the poor and unfortunate. But inside, in private, the person no one saw was Snow White. Demurely I walked the line of a perfect, trusting, unquestioning wife. My best friends were Dopey, Sleepy, Happy, Bashful, Sneezy, Grumpy and Doc; each one a mythical character, just like my life. I was singing as I walked the path to the poison apple, certain that my prince would come to awaken me.

CHAPTER TWELVE

Faith is a desperate dive out of the sinking boat of human effort and a
prayer that God will be there to pull us out of the water.

Max Lucado

Just weeks after we settled into our new home, a family moved
into the two-story colonial across the street. I met Joyce Kendall
one afternoon as we both stood outside enjoying the warm spring
weather. She walked over to my yard, introduced herself and
invited me to share a pot of tea. I accepted. Over the next several weeks, turning to months, Joyce and I drank gallons of tea
and talked about the myriad topics that at the time occupied our
minds; our children, clothes, food, travel, restaurants and inevitably religion.

Joyce was, by her definition, a Christian. She attended a
Nazarene Church. I knew nothing about a Nazarene Church and,
being a good, solid, albeit absent, Catholic girl, I remained skeptical. My years of Catholic upbringing raised red flags and sent
alarm bells screaming. The Nuns shouted in my head: *Stay away*
from this evil talk. The edicts from the Priests came flooding back:
You will be sent directly to Hell if you listen to this hearsay! And being a

well-trained Catholic girl, I was secure, if not smug, in my Catholic superiority.

"What do you mean saved?" I asked. "Saved from what?"

Our conversation had again drifted to religion, church, and God. Joyce's explanation of Salvation was so fundamentally foreign to me that she may as well have been speaking an alien language.

"The Bible tells us that we all fall short but God offers us His redeeming grace," she explained. "It's not something we can earn by being good enough or by working for it. It's the free gift of salvation through Jesus Christ. Jesus wants to have a personal relationship with each of us. He wants to come into your life, and mine, to forgive us all our sins." Joyce poured more tea for both of us as she spoke. "God sent His son, Jesus Christ, to do that on the cross."

"So, you're saying that I just make one trip to the altar for all my sins and I'm done?" I was not buying into the once for all program. The private confines of the Catholic confessional afforded me security. It was the preverbal pat on the head as a way to make me feel good again. It was incomprehensible to me that one trip to an altar could be a blanket of forgiveness.

"It's more than that," she said, "but basically, yes."

"But that's what confession is all about," I said. "And I can do it behind a dark curtain in the confessional." Growing up, I learned that anything to do with God was private, even secret.

"Christ tells us that we are separated from Him by our sins," she said. "He came and died on the cross, once and for all, so all our sins are atoned for, forever."

The idea of publically kneeling at an altar to ask forgiveness, screamed to me of awkward and embarrassing, two things I avoided at all costs.

"But what about the future?" I asked. "I'm going to do something, sooner or later that I know won't be according to God's laws. And what about the Priest?"

"That's what grace is all about," Joyce told me. "Christ knows that and loves you anyway. God tells us there is no mediator between God and man, except Jesus Christ."

My head was spinning. No Priest? Who would tell me what prayers to say for my penance? Until next time.

Later and alone, I thought about Joyce's words. I wanted her to be right. I desperately wanted to believe what she was telling me. Such love and grace, although alien to me, was something to be considered. My growing up years had taught me that love was conditional, a thing to be earned, often withheld due to forces beyond your control, and held in abeyance until earned again.

Sometimes, after listening to Joyce, I walked away believing she must be a bit weird, one of those crazy, holy-rolling, shouting religious persons. But I liked Joyce, and on the whole, she appeared sane and reasonable. Her kids were normal. Her husband seemed normal. All my good manners kicked in as I sat and listened politely, but kept my distance. Occasionally, I put forth one of my deep-seated, ingrained, rote Catholic arguments. The more I talked in Catholicism-speak, the hollower it sounded to my own ears. I admired Joyce's honest faith and trust in Christ. Her beliefs were not based on fear- fear of Hell, fear of rejection, fear of doing the wrong thing at the wrong time. She loved God and trusted Him, but did not fear Him.

Each Sunday morning the entire Kendall family left for church. Sunday evenings they went back to church. And on Wednesday nights, they went again. That was far too radical as far as I was concerned. I had stopped attending church altogether shortly after Danny and I married. Despite thinking the Kendalls were a bit strange for going to church so many times in one week, a part of me envied Joyce's faith. It was a faith I still did not fully understand or trust to be true, but could not deny that in Joyce's life it was genuine. I was slowly becoming aware of a gnawing inside me, a tiny hole somewhere that, despite all my efforts, remained empty. I worked diligently to ignore the echo it produced, but the sound only grew louder, reminding me that a part of me was empty and getting more so each day.

In the meantime, my quest to have another baby went on. During our move and becoming settled, my regular doctor visits became sporadic but the yearning for a baby did not diminish.

My daily ritual of taking my temperature continued as I filled out sheet after sheet of monthly charts. I stopped expecting anything to change but the thermometer under my tongue every morning was a comfortable habit.

And then, I was pregnant. After months, and now years of disappointments, I kept the news to myself until it was confirmed by a visit to my doctor.

"Well, congratulations, you did it," my doctor said. I sat in his office. The test result on my urine sample was positive, but given my history, he called me in for a physical exam before emphatically stating that I was pregnant.

"Wow," I said quietly. "Are you sure?"

"Oh yes," he laughed. "I suppose you're going to celebrate tonight?"

"No, I think I'll go to church." I said, surprised by own statement.

"Well, whatever you decide to do," he said, "make an appointment for next month. I want to get your pre-natal schedule set up."

"When am I due?" For days I asked myself that question, counting over and over again the weeks and months to come, anticipating holding another baby. The doctor and I discussed the due-date prediction.

I drove home cautiously allowing myself to think about being pregnant again. I practiced telling Dan the news. I envisioned us announcing to family and friends. There was no one in our circle who did not know of my struggle with infertility.

"Pregnant," I whispered the word aloud. I laughed. There was no one in the car to hear me speak the unbelievable news. Even now, all these years later, the emotions I experienced at that moment are as real and palpable to me as they were then. A life was growing inside me. Danny and I had created a life once again.

Danny was excited, Julie, now five years old, was thrilled and Michael smiled. We called family to make our announcement. Letting friends and neighbors know the fantastic news fell more to me because I could not wait for everyone to hear. I WAS PREGNANT!

Shortly after, I sat with friends talking about the pregnancy and my struggles to get to this point. Someone remarked, "After five years of trying, are you nervous that something might go wrong?"

Setting aside the callous stupidity of the remark, I paused to think. Finally I said, "If anything happens to this baby, they'll have to lock me away." Soon those words would reverberate in my head with mocking cruelty.

Two days later, the unthinkable happened. Waiting for surgery, hearing the words 'ectopic pregnancy, burst tube, no baby', my world now seemed a punishing cycle of give, only to lose once again. Life was a taunting thief, taking from me the things I cherished. I do not believe in curses, but at this point, I saw life as a heartless taskmaster, demanding of me every slender thread of peace and promise.

Following surgery, friends visited, each one tip-toing around the obvious. I had lost the baby. Danny's mother came to visit, offering sympathy and solace. Every visitor approached with trepidation, fearing what I would do after the devastating loss. I said nothing and only replied to their questions of how I was feeling with a non-committal answer. I was fortunate to be alive according to the doctors and that truth was only just sinking in for both Danny and me.

On my second day in the hospital Joyce came to visit me. She stood at my bedside and held my hand. I saw tears in her eyes. I blurted out, "Joyce, I met Jesus."

"What?"

"I met Jesus," I repeated. "He came and touched me, here," I put my hand on my shoulder, "when I was in the hallway waiting for surgery." I told Joyce the story of the emergency room, of being wheeled away screaming for help and the touch I felt. "He's real, Joyce," I said crying. "I know He's real." Joyce stayed with me, sitting down beside my bed as we talked. Her words from the weeks and months previously came back to me in a different way.

By the end of the week, I was released to go home. Walking upright was difficult. The surgeon's incision went from my naval straight down seven inches. When I jokingly complained to the surgeon that his incision was crooked, he said humorlessly, "We were trying to save your life, not give you a bikini belly." It was a reminder of just what had happened and of what could have been a much different outcome.

My discharge was allowed on condition that I rest and move slowly. Just seven days after surgery, I was still walking slowly and carefully, the incision still painful. And I was exhausted. There was no argument from me. As Dan wheeled me out the door, the doctor gave a parting instruction.

"There's no reason you cannot get pregnant again." He explained, "The surgeon removed the one tube, what was left of it, and one ovary, but left the remaining tube and ovary."

"But what happened? Why did the tube burst?" I asked.

"We don't know for certain. There was nothing left to be able to examine and find a cause," he said. "The tube had to have been blocked from infection or disease. Why, we will never know." He smiled, "Now go home and get pregnant."

That did not happen.

CHAPTER THIRTEEN

———⌾———

Could there be a more frightening fate than to realize just moments before your death that you have lived your entire life as someone else?
Paul Meier

Being home helped me heal physically. Having been touched by the hand of Jesus helped me heal emotionally. The pregnancy came and went so quickly, there were times it seemed unreal. Before long, I was back on the treadmill of testing, seeing new doctors, and relating my history from the beginning.

Fertility became an up and coming issue in the early 70s. Specialists opened offices at an alarming rate. New tests and better drugs appeared. I lined up for the privilege of trying each and every one offered. One of the new drugs at the time was Clomid, a pill designed to kick-start the ovaries, or in my case, ovary. According to my newest doctor, its side effect was possible multiple births. The pill prompted the ovary to spit out eggs at an alarming rate, or words to that effect.

Giving me the prescription, the doctor cautioned, "This could cause multiple births. You need to understand there is a real possibility of twins or even triplets."

Rather than giving me pause or being alarmed at the prospect of twins or triplets, I was ecstatic. Once again, my hopes soared. The memories of my surgery, the pain and fear and almost losing my life, all faded as I anticipated that this new *thing* was the answer I had been searching for.

Month after month had turned into year after year of disappointments. I blamed myself. It was my body and it would not do what it was supposed to do. I was angry. It was simply not fair that so many women, who already had several children, kept having more. At times the sadness overwhelmed me. I begged and pleaded with God. I bargained, promising all kinds of things if He would only give me another baby. Just as before, my every thought and action remained focused on getting pregnant. I ignored the miasmas swirling around me even as it grew.

The Clomid worked. My now familiar and constant companion, temperature chart, showed those crazy, wicked spikes of ovulation. But still, I was not pregnant. Sitting in front of my newest doctor, I listened to familiar words.

"There may be a blockage in the remaining tube," he said. "We'll have to check to be certain."

My heart sank. "They tried that before the ectopic," I told him, "and it didn't work."

"We do a different procedure now. One that isn't as invasive," he said. "It doesn't require a hospital stay or an anesthetic. We do it here in the office." He explained that instead of a dye, air would be pumped into the tube. "The accidental advantage of this procedure is, if there is even a slight blockage, the air could open the tube up." He assured me that the only side effect might be some slight pressure in my shoulders during the procedure and excess gas.

During my years of dealing with infertility, the many tests, procedures and drugs, I heard the same reassurance from each doctor, all male. Every one confidently asserting that there would be no pain, merely some discomfort. It did not matter the test or procedure, the smiling faces all spoke with confidence of ease and simplicity each time. Sitting here this time and listening to this doctor, I was remembering the second Hystosmpilgiogram I had months previously.

"Will I need someone to drive me to the hospital and home again after the test?" I was talking to the doctor on the telephone about the next day's procedure. He reassured me that it was a simple procedure and would take just over an hour. "The first time they did this *simple* procedure, I was admitted to the hospital and put under anesthetic," I told him, stressing the word *simple* and hoped my sarcasm was not wasted.

"Oh no," he said. "It's improved since then. It takes about an hour and you can drive yourself home." I was not convinced, but he was the professional.

I would be driving myself anyway. Although Dan wanted more children, the doctor visits, tests, and procedures were done on my own. He listened as I informed him, but his interest went no deeper than a nod of his head as acknowledgment. As in all aspects of my married life up to this point, I was on my own.

Once at the hospital out-patient admitting, the nurse gave me a hospital gown and instructed me to disrobe, putting the ties at the back.

"Leave your shoes on," she said. "Hang your clothes on the hook inside the changing stall." She recited the instructions without looking at me.

I walked into a large bathroom with several stalls and walked to the farthest one. I undressed, put on the ugly, threadbare hospital gown, ties in the back, and walked out with my navy blue strap pumps on my feet. Tears stung my eyes. I blinked them back. It was one more humiliating moment in a long line of demeaning moments of struggling with infertility. I was alone. No one waited in the waiting room for me.

A nurse helped me up onto the hard, cold table. Several people stood around the table, making connections, watching monitors and checking gauges. They spoke casually about various non-medical subjects. I was ignored, much as an inanimate object. No one acknowledged my presence or spoke my name. Someone placed my feet in cold stirrups and a sheet was draped over my legs. A television screen in the corner of the ceiling tilted towards the head of the table.

Speaking to me for the first time since entering the room, the doctor explained that I would see the dye go into my uterus and then flow out through the fallopian tube, assuming there was no blockage. I nodded that I understood but remained silent, my mouth clinched tight. I was shivering from cold and fear. As the process began, I felt pinching and pulling with increased cramping. And then I watched as the dye begin to flow, fill my uterus and, then into, and out of, the fallopian tube.

"Well that's good," the doctor told me. "Your tube is completely open. The ovary looks good." That was it. It was done. "You can hop down, get dressed and go home. You may feel some cramping as the dye works its way through your system, but nothing much."

The people in the operating room scattered, cleaning up and taking instruments away for cleaning. No one glanced my way as I got down off the table. A nurse told me that my doctor would get a written report by the following week.

I was already feeling more than some cramping as I put my feet over the side of the table. My navy blue strapped pumps setting next to the table looked ridiculous and out of place. I slipped them on and gingerly walked out of the room. No one noticed. Alone, inside the bathroom stall, I sat down on the toilet. Blood, mixed with dye rushed out and into the stool. I doubled over with cramps. No one came to check on me. After several minutes I managed to get dressed, walk to my car and drive myself home.

I sat in the driveway, waiting until the newest wave of cramping subsided so I could walk into the house. No one was home. Both Julie and Michael were at school and Danny was at work. I stumbled back to my bedroom, lay on the floor, curled into a fetal position and cried. The pain was dreadful but I was crying too, because I was alone on the floor. The cramping and bleeding lasted several hours.

Which was why, this doctor's assurance that it was a simple procedure with just a slight bit of discomfort did nothing to alleviate my hesitation. If he or any one of my previous doctors had possessed a uterus or ovaries, I may have been somewhat less skeptical. But still I said, "Okay, let's do it."

Weeks later and still not pregnant, Danny and I stood in our kitchen as he lectured me. I stood mute, head down in submission. Even with my head lowered, I was berating myself for being such a coward. Uttering a word in my own defense, or, the improbability of actually standing up for myself did not register in my thinking. It was more likely that an alien being from another planet would walk into the kitchen and join in our conversation.

"My mother said she does not feel welcome here," his voice rose with each word. "She told me you make her uncomfortable every time she comes to visit. What the hell is that about?" he demanded.

It was untrue, of course. I no more possessed the ability to cause her to feel uncomfortable than I could spit quarters. Neither was I capable of defending myself.

"I don't know what you're talking about," I said, already feeling guilty for something I knew nothing about. My heart pounded and my stomach tightened. I did not like Milly and did not trust her but I was also terrified of her and the absolute power she held over our lives. When Milly turned against you, there was cause for alarm.

Milly was cunning. Over the past several months I had noticed a cool feeling coming from her towards me. It was more than the indifference shown me in the past. This was a definite attitude shift. Repeatedly, I pushed the feeling aside, believing perhaps I imagined the new icy atmosphere. Even if I sought to understand it or question it, there was nowhere to look for answers. I had no family to turn to, my sister, Shirley Ann, lived with Milly. Making trouble of any kind would cause backlash to fall on her. Danny was no help or support. In his own way, he was as much her victim as the rest of those unfortunate enough to incur her displeasure. The world existed for Milly and that included her own children. I was genuinely frightened and felt cornered.

"Well, this better stop here and now," he demanded. As usual, I stood silent. I listened to his accusations, accepting that I must be guilty.

The day before Milly had telephoned Danny. She told him it was important they meet, privately, without Christine. He, of course, went as summoned. To deny Milly any request was unthinkable. You did not say no to her. It was at that lunch that she tearfully declared herself the target of my shrewish behavior. Playing the victim, an act I had witnessed firsthand too often in the past, Milly told her son how unhappy my thoughtless behavior made her. She felt shut out of Danny's life and did not understand why.

And now, having carefully loaded the gun, Milly gave it over to Dan. Predictably, as trained from his youth, Danny came home and let the shot be fired—at me.

"My mother and my sister are coming over this afternoon," he said. "You better not make her feel unwelcome," he pointed a finger at me. I knew my place. It had not changed and was not going to change. I was alone in this marriage.

Milly and Terry arrived a short time later. After a brief and triumphant hello, Milly suggested they, she, Danny and Terry, go into Michael's small bedroom to watch television. Without question, Danny led them to the bedroom and closed the door, leaving me standing alone in the kitchen. I stood there and let the door shut; closing me out of my own home, and I said nothing.

Later, I walked to the door and opened it. Danny, Milly and Terry sat watching the small television. "What are you doing?" I asked.

"We're watching TV," Danny said. Milly stared at me. "Can you close the door?"

I did as I was told. I hated her at that moment. But I also knew if she chose to end my marriage, it was already over. What I did not understand was why I had become the enemy. Her need for attention and control was obsessive and legendary but why she now needed to pull the cord on Dan and draw him into herself, was a mystery. Regardless of the reasons, real or imaginary, my time as wife was limited and I knew it.

Mr. Mrs. Pechacek, Leaving the Church

Shirley, Nick, Me, My Mom, Michael

*Wedding Party. L to R, Ron Heins,
Pam Prokuda, Lionel Lassiter,
Teresa, Me, Dan, Milly*

*On Our Honeymoon,
Niagara Falls, Canada*

Christine Pechacek

*My Mother and Stan On Their
Wedding Day, Fall of 1966*

*Me, Dan, Madison Heights,
baby shower for Julie, 1966*

Dan, Me and Julie, 1967

Julie and Me 1967

*1968 Me, Julie, Dan at home
in Madison Heights*

*Madison Heights., 1968 L to
R, Shirley Ann, Me in the back,
Teresa, Julie and Millie*

*Michael and Julie, Madison
Heights, 1968*

*The Ford Fairlane, Madison
Heights, 1968*

Our first new car, Pontiac LeMans,
1969, Madison Heights

Whitehouse Restaurant, Clare. Coffee
on the way to have Samuel, 1977

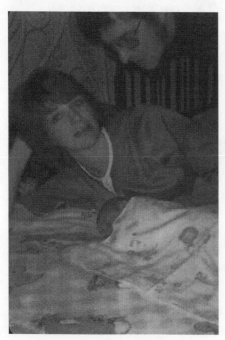

First day home with Samuel,
Me and Dan

Me with Samuel, 4 months old

Harrison, 1985, Family Portrait

Julie's Wedding Day, 1991

Samuel and Stacy, 2003 Wedding Day

*Repeating our vows on our 25th
Wedding Anniversary, May 21, 1991*

CHAPTER FOURTEEN

—◎◎◎—

There is no such raw material for songs that live from heart
to heart as that furnished by sorrow.

F.B. Meyer

It was July, just four months after my surgery. Physically I was back to normal. My scar, still red and tender, was a daily reminder that I was not pregnant. The doctors were out of ideas and I was bone-weary of new drugs that apparently did nothing but give me cramps, bloating or occasionally cause mysterious bumps and rashes to appear. But, stubbornly and out of desperation, I kept returning in the hopes that a new procedure or magic potion would appear. The most infuriating of all, however, was despite everything modern medicine offered nothing was found to tell me the why. I wanted to know and understand why, what was wrong with me. If there was no *thing* to be fixed, then there was no medicine, surgery or procedure to be employed that would bring this to an end.

One doctor suggested invetro-fertilization, a relatively new and expensive answer to infertility. Our insurance, which had covered one-hundred per cent of everything up to this point, drew the line at what was still considered experimental. For us to even consider incurring the cost, which at the time was $10,000, was out of the question.

I approached Danny with the idea of adoption. He neither discouraged my suggestion, nor did he encourage it. I called several adoption agencies. Each contact ended with no reassurances and little information. I was told because we had one child born to us, our position in line was last or not at all. In truth, I did not want to adopt. I wanted to become pregnant again and give birth.

All my previous arguments began to spring up like Old Faithful, in regular spurts of frenzy, whenever I made my plea to God. *I would be a good mother. We have a beautiful home and can provide for a child. It is not fair that women who do not want babies have them. So many children are neglected. I would not do that.* This I did on a regular basis and always accompanied by tears. But unlike Old Faithful gushing from its underground spring, my cries erupted from some empty place buried deep inside of me.

Dan and I were not close; at best, we shared a pseudo intimacy that masqueraded as marriage. On the outside our lives appeared stable, even comfortable. In truth, day by day we slipped further into living separate lives. I planted my feet firmly in my own world, denying any hint that our lives were not story-book perfect. Smiling to outsiders, I boasted about our marriage. We were happy. Danny was the perfect husband. I was extremely happy. They were all lies.

Danny lived his own life unhindered by me or those pesky marriage vows. I was a willing participant in the cruel ruse. I stopped asking questions and expected nothing other than what was apportioned out to me and delighting in his occasional favor. The cruel irony was that the farther I retreated from his world, believing the subterfuge for fear of the truth, the deeper his contempt for me became. I cowered. Danny became bolder. I accepted loneliness as a part of married life. Danny withdrew. The more I sought to be the perfect, never complaining wife, the more Dan fixated on a life away from me.

At the same time I remained on guard against any new hints of renewed intrusions from Dan's mother, Milly. No more had been said between us about how unwelcome she felt in my presence, but I was not stupid. Milly may have retreated from one minor skirmish, but if so it was to re-arm for the war. I smiled and agreed with anything and everything, fearful of giving Dan more reason to side with his mother against me. There was a war going on and, unfortunately, I was weaponless.

Shortly after my surgery Joyce had invited us to attend church with their family. Danny had become friends with Joyce's husband, Ralph and felt comfortable in going along. The Pastor, Reverend Howard Ricky, was a dynamic, energetic man and preached enthusiastically. His robust preaching was not bluster, smoke and mirrors. He seemed to sincerely love God and was driven by a desire to tell others. His preaching was sometimes humorous, always pointed and never veered from Biblical truthfulness.

One Sunday in July Dan and I sat with Joyce and Ralph near the front of the church. It was hot outside and inside the church. Air-conditioned churches were in the future as of yet. We sat near the front, close to a window. The men wore suits and ties and the women wore dresses, pantyhose, and high heels. I wore a multi-colored sheath dress made from a lightweight organza with heels just short of qualifying as stilettos. The dress was my own creation. I was hot and sticky along with most of the other women in the pews, but I looked good. Reverend Ricky, in a suit and tie, preached from the pulpit. As he finished he invited people to come to the altar for prayer.

Coming from a Catholic background, almost everything at this church was new and often strange. Altar calls, as they were referred to, were certainly at the top of that list. Joyce had explained the "getting saved thing" to me enough that it kind of made sense. Jesus Christ had come and died on the cross, which all good Catholics knew. I had grown up seeing Christ hanging on the big cross behind the priest every Sunday. He then arose and went to heaven. I understood and accepted both concepts as facts.

But, as Joyce explained to me over tea, there was more to it.

"Christ died for you personally. When he hung on the cross, it was for all your sins," she said. "Chris, Jesus wants to give you new life."

It was difficult for me to grasp that Christ's love and forgiveness required no effort on my part. My life to this point was predicated on my own efforts and careful planning. I raised logical arguments as Joyce told me about surrendering your life to Christ. Giving up control of any portion of myself alarmed me. I was living each day in a private chaos and to imagine giving up what little sense of control I had, however fragile, was unimaginable.

But like someone reading a sign that says *Hot! Do not touch!*, I had to know more. Was it possible that Jesus Christ could make a difference in my life? I was not good at trusting people, especially those closest to me. I wanted my life to change but each time I had opened a door, thinking the person knocking meant well for me, it was to find the tiger and not the lady.

But Joyce had said *new life*. I remembered that day in the hospital when Jesus touched me. That was new life. He saved my life.

Reverend Ricky's voice was inviting people to the altar for the prayer of salvation. I sat listening and thinking, *there is no way I am going up to that altar to make a public display of myself. Just stay put*, I told myself.

Inexplicably, I was on my feet, pushing past Joyce and Ralph to walk to the altar. I knelt down and began to cry.

Reverend Ricky knelt on one knee in front of me and quietly asked, "Why are you here Chris?"

"I'm not sure," I said between sobs. "But I feel so empty and afraid."

"Do you understand why Jesus came and what He did for you?" he asked.

"Yes."

"What is that Chris?"

"I'm a sinner but I know Jesus died for those sins and wants to set me free and save my soul. I want Him to forgive me." Tears ran down my face onto my dress. My words came rushing out. Reverend Ricky cried as he prayed for me.

Just a few pews back, still in the seat by Joyce and Ralph, Dan put his head in his hands. Another gentleman appeared, sat down beside him and said, "Would you like to go up there with your wife?" Tears ran down Dan's face. "I'll go with you if you want," Bob's voice was soft. Danny nodded and the two walked to the altar together. Danny knelt near me and prayed the same salvation prayer. He cried deep, wrenching sobs, his head bowed in prayer. Men from the church came to the altar and surrounded Dan, some kneeling and others standing nearby, they prayed with him. Their hands reached out to him, touching his back and shoulders, offering their love and support. We, husband and wife, left church that day born again, washed in the forgiving blood of Jesus Christ. We both walked away from that altar set free.

We went home but never sat face to face and shared our experiences, never opened that secret part in our hearts to let the other inside and see the fresh, tender bud of new life. Neither Dan nor I understood what intimacy meant. We did not comprehend it should be a part of what a husband and wife shared nor how fragile but vital intimacy was to marriage. We never witnessed it in our parents. Intimacy to us was the physical part of marriage. We could not fathom that true intimacy had nothing to do with sex. For us marriage was manipulation, arguing, fighting for control, secrets and lies. It was all we had known and seen portrayed throughout our growing years. The adults in our lives had spent all of their energy looking out for themselves, how they could get and then protect what was beneficial for their own life.

An opportunity for us to begin anew was lost in that moment when we each went off alone within ourselves and did not share our new found salvation.

An unfamiliar peace settled over me in the days that followed. The circumstances around me did not change, but I was changing. The strange void I felt for so long was silenced. Something was different, not eerie or strange, but soft and already familiar. I was genuinely happy but could not name the reason. It felt good.

Danny seemed to quickly forget his moment at the altar and his new salvation. His life went on as before, secrets and lies. The Enemy, seeing Dan's house momentarily swept clean, ran to get more demons and came back to securely dwell for a long time to come.

I believed that following Christ was my guarantee of a future free of lies, deceit and heartbreak. I was tragically ignorant. Hell was just around the corner, a sharp turn north.

CHAPTER FIFTEEN

—— ⊶⊷ ——

Anterior Cingulate Cortex (ACC): Weighs options, makes decisions. It's the worry-wort center [of the brain], and it's larger in women than in men.
Louann Brizendine, M.D.

It was the 70s. Home Interiors, Stanley Products, Tupperware and Toys. Inviting your friends over for a couple of hours, serving coffee, tea, and baked goods and demonstrating various products became common place. The various merchandise changed but the result was always the same. We purchased things we did not need, and then under concentrated pressure, booked a future party of our own.

Attempting to leave the party was akin to walking down a carnival midway. The female product demonstrator was good. Like the carnival barker, sensing the quarry about to slip out of reach, wheeled you in with, "If you book a party *today*, your friend will earn [win or receive] this wonderful free hostess gift." Sensing hesitancy or doubt, she added, "You know, she really wants this valuable item for herself." A pause to smile beseechingly, "If you book today, she will earn the extra points needed to do just that." And then leaning in closer, "Don't you want to help her?" We all caved in under the pressure.

Days later you found yourself sitting in the same circle of friends, listening to the same demonstrator drone on, selling the same useless items to the same women, none of whom needed anything being sold. The only things that did change were the products. And that was ruled by seasons.

In the late summer or early fall, Home Interiors was the focus of the neighborhood. After a few weeks of Home Interior buying, our homes began to resemble product showrooms. As I recall, sconces were a particularly popular item and a big seller, with red being the dominant color in candle choice. If by some chance, a softer effect was desired, then blue was your ticket. Blue and red were Home Interior hits. At one party I attended, having run through sconces, candles, pictures and fake flower streamers for the feminine touch, I resorted to buying a blue glass basket to set empty on the floor by a couch in our formal living room, where no one ever sat. I regularly picked the basket up and dusted it. It was unthinkable not to buy. If you expected the same friends to buy at the party you would be pressured to have, then you must buy from them.

Later in the fall it was toys. House to house we went over the weeks leading up to Christmas, oohing and aahing over cute, inventive and of course, educational toys. Each one a must for happy, satisfied children at Christmas.

Springtime was the time for cleaning, and nothing was better than Stanley Home Products for a respectable, clean, sparkling home. Following one get together of sharing these fine products with my dearest friends in my own home, I had a sudden break with reality. The demonstrator, or Nazi Storm Trooper as I preferred to call her, convinced me I was perfectly suited to sell Stanley Home Products.

"You are so friendly," she cooed. "I can see that these ladies look up to you. And that's understandable. You are a charming woman." She paused for that to sink in and added, "I know you would do well as a demonstrator and earn money for so little of your time." I stared at her not yet convinced. Then the final stab, "I bet you could be a top seller and make big profits." Ca-ching!

Ca-ching! The prospect of money and being successful was the lasso that snagged, tagged and dragged me down.

The next week, accompanied by my recruiter, I sat in a large meeting room in a cheap hotel. Scores of women had come together for what was a monthly pep rally. I was seated in the front row, making an early escape less likely once the rally got underway. And it did. Balloons floated over the audience of women, streamers floated from the ceiling and Stanley posters plastered the walls. The room full of enthusiastic women clapped furiously to the beat of the deafening music blasting from several loud speakers situated around the room.

I stood, starring, not quite believing the bazaar spectacle. Following several minutes of deafening music, the meeting was called to order. My front row seat sandwiched me between two exuberant ladies who extolled the Stanley life.

"You are going to love selling Stanley," one smiling lady told me. I backed away as she leaned into my face.

From my other side a face appeared, "Oh you know Stanley just sells itself. It's just that wonderful."

Running from the room crossed my mind. Sitting newcomers in the front row was a wise decision on the planners' part. I felt trapped. The meeting progressed with what I expected, new product information and hype, sales goals for the next month and upcoming events.

So far I was still mildly interested. The female frenzy and squealing was definitely a turnoff but I was determined to see it through. After all, I possessed this charm that could spiral me to earn thousands of dollars and, all for just one or two evenings a week. What could be simpler?

"Okay ladies," the woman in front of the room shouted. "This is it." The women began muttering and shuffling in their seats. The crowd was winding up. But for what, I wondered.

"It's that time once again!" More clapping and shouting from the crowd. "Our top Stanley girl of the month!" Her voice rose to a crescendo.

The throng of wide-eyed women stood, some knocking over chairs in their frenzy. The applause drowned the speaker's voice. Not to be outdone, she grabbed a microphone.

"And she is," she paused for dramatic effect, "Mary!" Shrieks, thunderous applause and jumping up and down broke out. "Come on up Mary!" She screamed into the microphone. No one was listening. Every eye searched the aisle, waiting for Mary to appear.

Mary came running to the front of the room, clapping and laughing. I did not see tears but it seemed at one point that Mary might hyperventilate from the excitement. I hoped someone had a paper bag for Mary. My plan of getting rich quick evaporated in a jolt of reality. These women are crazy, I thought to myself. Any semblance of an idea I held of selling Stanley Products vanished in a panicked flash. My only thought was escape. If I thought it could not get any worse, I was wrong.

Mary received a prize for her month's success and got to ring a bell. A large bell was handed to Mary. She needed both hands to raise the massive piece of iron up and over her head before swinging it back and forth.

Gong! Gong! The awful sound rang out, echoing in my ears. The women, now glassy-eyed and zombie-like, chanted, "Ring the bell for Mary! Ring the bell for Mary!"

I was fortunate to escape with my life as far as I was concerned. Charm be damned. I would never be a Stanley girl. Sadly, I would never get to ring the bell and hear, "Ring the bell for Chris!"

That was a close call.

The 70s was also the decade of decoupage. Crafters burned the edges of pictures, poems, letters and various other paper keepsakes, all to give the appearance of a treasured heirloom. These charred items were then glued to wood pieces of various sizes and shapes and slapped with enough urethane to keep several large men high for a month. The result being blocks of shining wood hanging on the walls of every home you entered, right next to the Home Interior sconces filled with red or blue burning candles.

Decoupage was not my talent. I had no interest in crafts and certainly not in making my own.

Reading was a sport for me. I read volumes of books. One summer I read through all of Agatha Christie. My summers in Sterling Heights also began my romance novel period, old world, Victorian romances. They were not filled with graphic sex or violence. In these the heroine was loved and cherished by the strong hero. She inevitably cast herself on his great, loyal strength and was embraced by his devotion and power. Not to mention that he was of course stunningly handsome. It was a world I desired, but did not possess.

My husband was not my hero and I was not cherished. Casting myself on Dan's anything would have and often did, result in me hitting the floor—alone. Danny, a good financial provider, was simply absent as a husband, a lover or even companion. Reading and becoming lost in the innocent love and romance of the novels filled a need in my life I did not understand or realize even existed. As the months and years passed, the hole became a gaping wound until finally, a chasm opened up and we both fell in, lost. We had become strangers. I was in a hole so dark and so foreboding, there were no words to describe what I felt or experienced. I did not understand it myself, so deep were the lies I told myself. Lost in my make believe world of a loving husband and perfect marriage, Dan saw it as his ticket to a life of single freedom. He believed himself permanently stamped with a get out of jail card free.

I kept stamping the damn thing myself. I nodded, I smiled, I cooed, I agreed with him in all things, giving my naïve stamp of approval. Fear kept me quiet. Fear of being abandoned kept me blind. Fear of confrontation kept me imprisoned. Fear that I was not good enough kept me in a prison of implicit approval.

CHAPTER SIXTEEN

———— ∞∞ ————

Violence and injury enclose in their net all that do such things, and
generally return upon him who began.

Lucretius

The husbands and wives we met at Bethel Nazarene Church became the majority of our social life. Following our salvation and now regular church attendance, the men and women of the church reached out to us in genuine caring and made me feel a part of their group.

Dan fit comfortably with the men whatever the topic of conversation. His charm and affable manner radiated to magically draw people into his web. At home, away from the spotlight, alone with me, a different Dan appeared. As had become his practice, Dan was secretive, putting him on the periphery of our lives; his and mine. If asked, I could not name or identify what it was that existed between us. But I knew it covered us as an impenetrable fog; carefully maneuvering but never touching. He afforded me his physical presence but little else. Much like a visiting statesman, he occasionally attended to necessary matters; me.

Each Sunday, following the evening service, we were invited to an informal get together at another couple's home. There was a small meal, usually sandwiches and a dessert. There was no liquor, beer, coarse joking or backbiting by the women. This new atmosphere made me feel welcome and at ease.

In our former circle of friends, the atmosphere had been a continuing undercurrent of menace. It was not a place where I felt safe from the barbs of the people around me. I did not trust the women. I had engaged in the gossip and rumor mongering myself, flinging the juicy tidbits and innuendos in full abandon. I reasoned that it was justified because it afforded me inclusion into the group. It was an invention of my own to lessen the guilt I experienced as I tattered another person's reputation. Of course, I knew that the same things were inflicted upon me. What I had not done or even considered was making myself available to someone else's husband. However, that was a common occurrence in our former neighborhood. Sadly, leaving the physical space of Madison Heights did not alter the behavior of some I had considered friends.

As a couple, Dan and I assumed we knew how to have fun. We went to parties, drank with our friends, and joined in with the usual party behavior. An evening with our new church friends brought new meaning to the words *fun* and *party*. We joked and laughed about clean, healthy things. The women did not gossip. The men did not separate from the group and drink beer, watch sports on television or whisper off-color jokes.

The first New Year's Eve we spent with our new friends was at a house party hosted by Jackie, a lovely woman and gracious hostess, and her husband, Bob. They lived in a large two-story colonial home. Jackie utilized each room of the first floor for food and games. Fondue was the rage in the late 70s.

Every woman I was acquainted with served a fondue to satisfy the discriminating palates of her guests. Along with the fashionable Home Interiors décor and various decoupage wooden pieces hanging everywhere, we had fondue.

For her New Year's Eve party, Jackie served a meat station, a cheese station and the final one, a chocolate fondue for dessert. We wandered room to room eating and playing various games Jackie had set out. We numbered forty that night. The house rocked with merriment. It was contagious. Screaming laughter wafted from room to room. As midnight approached, we heard pounding on the front door. A crowd of us went to the door. Two uniformed officers stood on Jackie's front porch.

"Ma'am, we received a complaint from some of your neighbors," one officer said to Jackie. We all laughed. "They are complaining about the noise. You will have to keep it down." This brought more laughter and squeals from us.

"Oh, gosh, officer, we are so sorry," Jackie said. "We will really try to tone it down." We laughed harder.

"May I caution you as well that your guests should not attempt to drive home if they have had a little too much to drink? It's not a wise thing to do." His gentle, respectful warning brought a fresh bout of laughter and squealing.

Gaining control of herself and us, Jackie said, "Officer, there is no alcohol here. We don't drink. We're a church group. It's just us having a good time."

The officers looked at each other, both smiled and said, "Well, in that case, Ma'am, have a great night. And keep on laughing. Happy New Year."

As they turned to leave, we all screamed "Happy New Year!" Jackie closed the door and the party continued. That night taught me something valuable. When God's people get together, it is wonderful to be around them. I was now a part of that group. I felt a part of something unique, a place where I now belonged. A beginning opened up for me.

Dan joined in enthusiastically, becoming who he needed to be for the crowd he was with at the time. It was one of the many masks he so successfully wore and as easily removed. I remained but one part of the masquerade. His mask of *husband* did not interfere with his other life. Amazingly, Danny was capable of living two lives with impunity. He expertly lived as two separate persons. His expertise at keeping them separate for decades testifies to the callousness he had built up over time. And to the almost total destruction it brought to his heart and soul.

Dan and I had established a firm pattern for our marriage. We rarely spoke of anything other than the everyday and the mundane. What bills must be paid. What, if any, plans might we have for a weekend. What was going on with the kids and school. Should we buy new furniture. There were no discussions of hopes, dreams or the window to our souls. For me to do so would have been futile. Danny obsessively guarded his secret world. He did not speak casually or offhandedly for fear that a casual remark would fail to line up with previous lies. Just as a moat and drawbridge guard a castle, Dan's silence protected him. I asked no questions. Casual curiosity was met with anger. Eventually I stopped talking. That was how we lived. It was a miserable existence for both of us. It was a life full of lies and corruption, but it was the only way we knew to live as man and wife.

Danny grew up in a house of lies, cheating and adultery. Both his father and mother were experts at deception. All their attention had been focused on themselves to the exclusion of all else, and most pointedly, their children. For my part, I grew up in anger and abuse. My father controlled us all by fury. My mother, weak and frightened, lived helplessly in its grip. I had no more been the focus of my parents' lives than had Dan. From this, Danny and I foolishly believed we had come away unscathed. Our lives had been and continued to be a cruel irony. We became what we reviled.

We each learned early in life to keep the secret part of our hearts locked and guarded. I lived terrified of being trampled, crushed and lost should I dare to open my heart. I witnessed the destruction vulnerability brought to my mother. Dan learned as a young boy that the world was a dangerous place for openness and honesty. He learned to seal off the vulnerable portion of his heart. It was better and safer to run, and to lie in order to survive. He was on his own in the labyrinth of cruelty his parents had created.

Our church friends provided a safe, loving world where we relaxed, laughed and for brief snippets in time, pretended to be a loving, committed couple. To outsiders Dan and Chris were an attractive couple, good parents and had a picture perfect marriage.

Couples outside of church occasionally crossed our paths and we would, for a time, have brief friendships. Pete and Evelyn* were two such people. Dan met Pete, also a sheet metal journeyman, on a job. They struck up an acquaintance. After several weeks, Evelyn, Pete's wife, called and invited us over on a Saturday night to play cards. Evelyn said they planned to barbeque and maybe later in the evening take a swim in their pool, and to remember to bring our bathing suits. I said that sounded like fun.

The next Saturday we arrived at Pete and Evelyn's home at the agreed upon time. We ate and played a game of cards. It was not a roaring good time but we were enjoying ourselves.

So far.

As the evening wore on Pete suggested a moonlight swim in the backyard pool. Evelyn showed us a spare bedroom where we could change into our bathing suits and provided us each with a towel. Dan and I changed and went out to the backyard. The moon was full and it provided a soft glow over the yard and the pool. Pete and Evelyn were already in the pool.

"Come on in," Pete said. "The water is really warm tonight." It had been hot earlier in the day and the sun had warmed the otherwise cool pool water.

Dan and I climbed into the refreshing water. We stood awkwardly for a few minutes, our backs resting against the wall of the pool. The above ground pool was round and about twenty-four foot in diameter. We began talking quietly, dipping in and out of the water, and enjoying the refreshing feel.

From the other side of the pool, Dan and I heard Evelyn begin to laugh softly. Then we heard, "Oh Pete, stop that. You're being naughty." Something flew across the pool and landed in front of Danny. He reached out to grab whatever it was and held up a bathing suit bottom. It was Evelyn's. As calmly as I could without making a scene, I got out of the pool. Dan was right behind me. We had no idea what precipitated the move by Pete and we did not ask questions. I thought the prank, or whatever Pete meant it to be, was inappropriate. And said so to Dan.

"What the heck was that all about?" I said as we changed back into our clothes in the same small spare bedroom. Dan had no answer and just shrugged. "Why would a man do that to his wife? In front of other people?" I was incredulous. We should have left then. But we did not and agreed to stay and play cards again. Not another word was said about Evelyn's bathing suit bottom flying across the pool and landing in front of my husband.

"Hey, Dan, want to make a quick run to the store with me for some beer?" Pete grabbed his wallet and keys as he headed to the door. Dan followed out the door.

As soon as the door was closed, Evelyn said in a hushed voice, "Chris, I want to show you something." She motioned for me to follow her down the hall to the master bedroom "I want you to see something. Pete has been collecting these for months," she said as she bent over to open the bottom drawer of a large dresser. "Tell me what you think."

The drawer was large, both deep and wide. It was filled to the top with magazines. I leaned in closer. The covers of the magazines all faced up. Each magazine was about swingers, as they were called in the 70s. Along with the fondue fad, the newest thing to hit the suburbs was wife-swapping. Although I had heard about this new practice, I did not believe it actually existed. It was incomprehensible. Admittedly, I was inexperienced, even innocent, but this went beyond naïveté.

The magazine covers glaring up at me from the drawer were revoltingly graphic. Even a quick glance showed naked bodies, arms and legs entangled in groups, showing a mass of naked flesh. It was not pretty. If Evelyn's plan was intended as an inducement for me to say, "Gosh that looks like fun" She was sorely disappointed.

"Good grief," I said. "Those are disgusting." I turned to look at Evelyn. "Doesn't that bother you that he keeps this garbage?" My first thought was that the magazines and their subject matter were as appalling to Evelyn as to me. Then, I was remembering the bathing suit bottom almost hitting my husband in the face.

Evelyn was quiet, looking closely at me for my reaction. I gave it to her. "How can you even allow that garbage in your house? What if one of your kids finds this? How can you let Pete touch you after looking at this garbage? Oh, is this what Pete wants? He wants you to participate in this filth? I'd shoot Dan if he suggested this to me." My words came out in one long rush. Evelyn silently closed the drawer and we walked back to the kitchen.

We made small talk while we waited for Pete and Dan to return with the beer. It was awkward for us both. After someone makes known to you that she is willing, and eager to have sex with your husband while, at the same time, you have sex with her husband, the conversational tone grows hollow in comparison. Evelyn did not say anything more about the drawer full of magazines. I had said enough. Within minutes, Pete and Dan were back. I told Dan I was ready to go home.

"Really? So soon?" Pete was disappointed. I was betting he was. Pete was in no way attractive, but now, looking at him made my skin crawl.

"Yes," I grabbed Dan's hand and headed for the door. "I'm really tired and we need to get home to check on the kids."

"Okay, well, let's do this again soon," Evelyn told us as we walked out the door. I was ahead of Dan on my way to the car.

Once in the car, I told Dan what had happened and what Evelyn showed me. "What?" he looked at me at he backed out of the driveway. "Are you kidding?"

"No, I am not kidding. Did you know Pete was like that?"

"Chris, give me some credit. No, I didn't know that, but it does explain the stunt in the pool."

"Well, they give me the creeps now."

"Absolutely," Dan said emphatically. "I'm not sharing my wife with another man. That really is twisted."

That brief episode, and the short-lived acquaintance with Pete and Evelyn, ended our almost encounter with the wild side of the 70s and wife swapping.

CHAPTER SEVENTEEN

He satisfies all instincts which He has implanted. He harkens to every cry which He has instilled. And, therefore, with unerring love and power He will respond to every appeal made to Him by his suffering ones.

F.B. Meyer

I was married and I was alone much of the time. Consequently, I had copious amounts of free time. I cooked, cleaned, shopped for groceries, and made myself a visible parent at Julie's elementary school. My goal was, of course, to be valued and appreciated. My new friends, the women of our new church, were active in various things and I became a part of their activities as well. We occasionally went to lunch, often meeting in someone's home. I joined Bible study groups. I began reading a Bible. I read books about studying the Bible, and books about how to pray. My experience with prayer was what I had learned growing up Catholic. We recited rote prayers, written long ago by someone, somewhere. As I spent time with the ladies from church and in their Bible study groups, I experienced a fervency and sincerity I had not seen before. When they prayed, it was spontaneous and heartfelt. They talked to God. I heard their heart in the words. It was personal and real.

"I didn't think you owned a Bible, so I thought I would buy you your first," Joyce said as she handed me a small box. Inside the box was a black leather King James Bible. It was the first Bible I had ever owned, but far from the last. Over the years I have purchased many, various versions, leather, and cloth, from large to pocket-sized. Each one carries a piece of me. They are a biography of my growth, my struggles and disappointments. I recorded doubts, failures and triumphs. Anyone leafing through the pages would read of the times I was angry at God, railing against Him for my sorrow and pain, and expressing my trust in Him. Looking back, I am grateful for the person who, many years ago, told me to write in my Bible.

"Thank you very much." Without waiting, I opened the soft leather cover and began flipping through the pages.

"You need to read it every day," Joyce said. "And pray every day." I began that day to do exactly what Joyce told me and have continued throughout the years with few exceptions. The rare prolonged periods of not doing so mark the times I was angry at God for the hurts in my life. Like a petulant child, I turned my face to the wall and pouted, thinking to teach God a lesson.

My unceasing battle to become pregnant gave me a focus and a reason to look to a happier future. I remained convinced if I gave Dan a son, he would see my value and love me in a deeper way. As I had when I was a child and wanted to marry Danny, I turned myself to pray about it. This time, however, the prayer was going to be a personal conversation with God.

Late one night, lying in bed next to my sleeping husband, I prayed silently. I told God the whole story. I had tried everything I knew, I reminded God. I reiterated to God of tramping from doctor to doctor, being poked and prodded, having test after test, all to no avail. The heavy sense of powerlessness felt darker than ever before. I allowed my mind to consider that I would never become pregnant, that I would never hold a newborn son in my arms. It frightened me and a sense of sadness I had not experienced before engulfed me. A palpable dread as real as the dark outside my bedroom window covered me. I had staked my entire worth as a wife on bearing a son. I believed that if I did not have that, then I had nothing. I would have nothing of value to offer Dan. He did not see me as a cherished part of his life. I was desperate to bring something treasured into our lives. It must be a thing more valuable than the momentary thrills that enticed him now. Obviously, just me was not doing it.

Quietly, I slid out of bed, knelt at the bedside, put my face in my hands and began to pray. "Lord, please tell me if I am ever going to have another baby." I whispered. "You know I want a son. I want it more for my husband than I can tell you." I waited.

For the first time in my life, I was not just talking to a distant ethereal God; someone I did not know and probably had not believed in with any genuine belief. But now it was different. He was not the far off and distant God I feared as a child. I listened week after week to preaching about hearing from God and was still unsure what that meant. I did not believe that a disembodied voice would boom from the sky, but I did expect something tangible. I stayed on my knees and waited. In the stillness and the soft glow of the bedside lamp, I suddenly understood that for the first time, I was at a pivotal point. I not only wanted an answer, I was ready for an answer. Whatever the answer might be.

I prayed, "God, if I am going to have another baby, tell me. If I'm not, tell me that so I can get on with my life." And then, "I will accept what you say." Once the whispered words were out of my mouth, I realized their finality. My life was going to change after tonight, of that I was certain. An unexpected calm spread through me. Good or bad, right or wrong, it was no longer up to me. I was not bargaining with God. This was not an, if you, then I, prayer. This was me, standing before God, and giving control to Him.

Making those two statements was for me, the most vulnerable thing I had ever done. For the first time, I was unconditionally giving up control of my life and body. I surrendered the deepest desire of my heart. I crawled back into bed and sat up. I picked up my Bible. It was *The Living Bible*, a new version just released, written in everyday language. I knew that once and for all, my answer was here, tonight. I hesitated and looked up to the ceiling. I was determined to keep my end of the prayer just uttered. Yes or no, it would be God's answer. Taking a deep breath, I placed my hands on the cover and randomly opened it. Looking down at the page, I saw *I Samuel, Chapter One*. This was new to me. Most of my reading in the Bible was in the New Testament. This was Old Testament stuff. Still, this was where the pages fell.

> *This is the story of Elkanah. . .. He had two wives, Hannah and Peninnah. Peninnah had some children, but Hannah did not. Each year Elkanah and his families journeyed to the Tabernacle to worship the Lord of the heavens and to sacrifice to Him. . .Elkanah would celebrate the happy occasion by giving presents to Peninnah and her children but although he loved Hannah very much, he could give her only one present, for the Lord has sealed her womb; so she had no children to give presents to. Peninnah made matters worse by taunting Hannah because of her barrenness. Every year it was the same—Peninah scoffing and laughing at her as they went to Shiloh, making her cry so much she couldn't eat"* (I Samuel: 1:1-7, TLB).

My stomach tightened. I closed my eyes, afraid to read further. It seemed God's answer was a no. Still, I had told God it was up to him and I would not go back on my word. I kept reading.

> *One evening after supper, when they were at Shiloh, Hannah went over to the Tabernacle. Eli the priest was sitting at his customary place beside the entrance. She was in deep anguish and was crying bitterly as she prayed to the Lord. And she made this vow, "Oh Lord of heaven, if you will look down upon my sorrow and answer my prayer and give me a son, then I will give him back to you, and he'll be yours for his entire lifetime..."*
>
> *Eli noticed her mouth moving as she was praying silently and, hearing no sound, thought she had been drinking.*

"Must you come here drunk?" he demanded. "Throw away your bottle."

"Oh no, sir!" she replied, I'm not drunk. But I am very sad and I was pouring my heart to the Lord. Please don't think that I am just some drunken bum!"

"In that case, cheer up! May the Lord of Israel grant you your petition, whatever it is" (I Samuel 1:9-17, TLB).

A son. Hannah asked specifically for a son. Just like me. And God answered her prayer. That was it. There was my answer. It was a long time before I fell asleep. I was ecstatic. I was going to have a son. And I even had his name, Samuel. God told me Himself. I did not have a date, but it was a fact, nonetheless. In my mind I was as good as pregnant. I fell asleep listing all the people I was going to tell my exciting news. Even today, so many years later, I marvel at how, in one instant, God sealed this promise in my heart, protected from doubt and the enemy's accusations.

Hesitantly, I told Dan. My faith was new and raw. I was still shy in discussing anything to do with prayer, God and how real my relationship with Jesus was becoming, especially with Danny. I remained desperate for my husband's approval and feared looking foolish in his eyes. Predictably, he was less than enthusiastic. His reply was a nod of his head and a brief, okay. I told him the whole story of the night before, thinking if he knew this was straight from God, he might be more excited. He did not share my euphoria. Instead, I received another non-committal nod, and "That would be nice. I hope you're right."

"Oh, I'm right." I said. "God said it. He promised me." Still less than animated over my revelation, I told him, "You just wait and see. I'm right. I know I am."

I walked away feeling the preverbal pat on the head, acknowledging the little girl's belief in Santa, the Easter bunny and the tooth fairy. But, Dan's lack of belief in God's promise to me did nothing to deter me from eagerly anticipating the future birth of my son, Samuel. I knew what I knew. I had gotten the words straight from the Lord. And He never lies. Neither is God capricious.

Friends smiled and said that it was nice that I believed in this thing. Our friends at church expressed encouragement, reminding me to read the Bible and keep praying. Not spoken, but implicit in their words, was a caution that I not go off the deep end. Family members said little. It did not matter to me what anyone else thought or believed. I knew the truth. If God and I were going to be the only ones who stayed excited for my son's birth that was okay with me. I did not waver. I did not doubt. In the months and even years of waiting, I did not let go of the promise, nor of my faith in the promise giver. My son, Samuel, was as good as in my arms. It simply did not occur to me that God could not do what He promised.

CHAPTER EIGHTEEN

———— ✦ ————

Say yes and you'll figure it out afterward.

Tina Fey

Julie was in first grade and Michael, now in high school, was increasingly self-sufficient. Dan, as was his practice, lived his life comfortably as much apart from our lives as he could possibly manage and still give the appearance of being a husband and father. I accepted each day as it was.

Dan and I talked of selling our house in Sterling Heights and moving north. It had been an on and off subject for a couple of years. Like many city dwellers, we saw the constant and rapid growth around us and wanted no part of it. My sister and her husband lived in Harrison and visiting them gave us positive impressions of that city and the surrounding areas. We decided to make the move and went forward with a plan. Dan was confident that he would find a company to work for in the northern part of the state.

Our first step was to find property. Our visits to Milly and her husband, Bill, culminated in property searches. Bill, a lifelong resident of the area, and my sister's husband, Lowery, knew the county well. On one weekend search, Lowery showed Dan a fifteen acre parcel north of Harrison. Lowery had thought to purchase the property himself but decided against it. He offered to show it to Dan. It was wooded with a stream running through and had an ideal spot for a house. He then took Bill and his mother to view the property. Lastly, he showed it to me.

"I really like this property," he told me the following weekend. We had driven back up north to walk the area more thoroughly. "I wanted you to see it before we made any decisions."

"I like it," I told him as we stood atop a slight rise not far off the dirt road. "This spot, right here is perfect for a house, just far enough off the road."

We stood surveying the landscape, and making plans for where a house would stand. The decision was made to purchase the fifteen acres for the asking price of $5000.00. At that precise moment, we did not have the full amount. As had been our practice since becoming engaged and continuing as a married couple, we saved money on a weekly basis. In money matters, we were both disciplined and practical.

Milly and Bill came to us with an offer. They would purchase the property and we would make monthly payments to them, sans interest. We agreed but also made immediate plans to, as quickly as possible, pay the balance. Other than our house payment and car payment, we had no debt. Paying cash for purchases was something on which we both remained resolute. The property purchase was no exception. As I had done prior to our wedding, I would get a job and my checks would go into a savings account to pay for the property. Once the property was paid for in full, we would proceed with the next step, selling the house and making the move. This is how I came to work at the Sterling Heights Medical Clinic and to meet Linda Silver.

Once the plan was decided upon, I began job hunting. Other than a high school diploma, I possessed no special skills. My only other employment had been at Becker's Meet Market and Bakery. Thankfully, there were no meat markets in Sterling Heights. I looked at want ads, sent in applications, and made phone calls to various places but nothing materialized. Prayer was a very real part of my life now so I set out to pray for a job.

"Lord, you know I want to work so that we can pay off this debt. And I am doing all I know to do." I was sitting with my Bible one morning, alone. "God, please help me find a job." And so there would be no misunderstanding between me and God, I added, "I will work anywhere but at a doctor's office." I had no desire to be around sick people. As I was to quickly learn, God has a heightened sense of humor.

Because nothing developed, despite my telephone calls and searching the want ads, I decided to go personally and ask for a job. One particular day, I dressed up, got in the car and drove up and down Van Dyke Avenue looking for businesses. Just two miles from our house was a brand new office complex, Sterling Heights Medical Clinic. The complex itself took up a block square. Driving into the parking lot, I assured myself that they must have some sort of office work I could do. After all, I had told God that I would not work for an actual doctor. And I was confident that God knew my logic to be sound.

I parked my car, and walked through the main doors. The immediate area was one gigantic waiting room. Off to one side were several smaller rooms, walled off by glass, with a large desk and accompanying office tools; typewriter, telephone, copy machine, and file cabinets. Directly at the back of the main area was a long desk with a privacy front facing the reception area. Sitting at the desk was a receptionist. I walked to the woman sitting behind the mini wall.

"May I help you?" She was young and perky. Perky irritates me.

"Yes, you can," I said. "Are there any jobs available?" We smiled at each other. Wearing my pseudo-confident mask taxed my energy. The role of self-assured female required pre-planning and looking the part was paramount. I wore a soft pale blue body-hugging knit dress with long-sleeves and a turtle neck. The hemline fell just above my knees. I wore black high heeled shoes that made my long legs appear longer still. My mirror told me I was drop-dead gorgeous. But like Snow White, the same mirror reflected that poison apple waiting for me to take a bite.

"Well, I can ask. But in the meantime, I can have you fill out this application." Again, a big smile.

I took the application form she held out to me, shot another one of my sunny smiles her way and went to sit down in one of the comfortable chairs. Pen in hand, I worked at filling out the application. My lack of employment experience made filling out the form an easy task. I was tired of filling out the same blanks, answering the same questions and then walking away never to hear from anyone. And I did not want to work in this place anyway. By the time I finished with the application, I had attitude.

The perky receptionist was on the telephone when I walked back to her desk. I waited. She hung up, turned to me and smiled. That smile was beginning to piss me off. I handed her the paper.

"Okay, thank you. Someone will call you." I considered slapping that grin off her face but refrained. I was discouraged and beginning to work up a whapping pity party for myself. I wanted to go home and retreat into my quiet world.

I am not sure where it came from, but I said, "No." Smiling girl looked at me and part of the smile faded. "No, I want to talk to someone today, now. If no one can see me, then I will take my application back and leave." I stared at her.

She got up and walked away into one of the glass-walled offices. She spoke to a man sitting at one of the desks. He listened and looked my way. I stared back. I was tired, my feet hurt and the whole job search thing was physically painful for me. It was exhausting to put on my confident face, even for short periods of time. Forcing myself to pretend I was bold and confident was draining.

Smiling girl came back and ushered me into the same office. The man stood, put out his hand and introduced himself as the facility director. We shook hands and I sat down. Over the course of the next hour, I convinced this man that actual experience did not matter. I was intelligent, energetic and capable of learning any job he might offer me. My act, my pale blue body-hugging dress and long legs worked because I left with a job. I would be working full time as a receptionist—for three general practitioners. I was certain I heard God chuckle and my guardian angel say, "Good one, Lord."

Two days later I arrived, dressed in nurse whites, white hose and shoes, for my first day on the job. The clinic was a labyrinth of offices connected by a maze of hallways. Each office, some twenty of them, housed separate practices, doctors, and nurses, each with their own receptionist. The receptionist desk set directly inside the door of one of the offices.

"There are three doctors here, each has their own nurse, but you are the sole receptionist for this area." The director of nursing was explaining the job and my particular duties. "You will answer the phones, take messages, relay information to the nurse in charge and keep the three appointment books."

There were six small exam rooms within the office area. Doors kept opening and closing; a nurse came out occasionally, retrieved something and went back into the exam room. Then a doctor came out, grabbed a new chart and went into the next room. No one took note of the new receptionist. I watched all the activity and felt a small panic bubble beginning to move up my throat. Swallowing hard, I forced a smile at the nursing director.

"Well, I'll leave it to you for now. If you have any questions, just give me a shout. My office is down the hall." With that, she was gone. The bubble was becoming the Hindenburg.

A tall, long-legged red head flew out of one of the rooms. She was the nurse to one of the three doctors. "Oh hell," the red-head said under her breath. And, "Idiot." She walked to the cupboards behind my desk, opened one and began to search for something. Turning to look directly at me, she said, "Hi. You must be the new gal." She was tall, close to six foot, with blue eyes, and shoulder length red hair.

"Yes," I said, "I just got here. My name is Chris."

"I'm Linda Silver," she tilted her head to the door of the room she had just left, "and the idiot in there is my doc." As Linda finished her introduction, the doctor she referred to came out of the small exam room. He was young, not tall, certainly not tall standing next to Linda's six foot frame, with sandy, unruly hair.

He grinned at Linda, "You call him. I don't want to." Linda picked up the desk phone, a beige rotary model, and threw it at him across the room. He laughed and went into the next exam room. I sat riveted to my chair, mouth open, waiting to see what happened next.

"Do you believe he wants me to call his patient and tell him he has cancer?" And then more to herself than to me, "Ass-hole."

That was my first introduction to Linda Silver. We became immediate friends. Linda was crazy, fun, smart, and never took life too seriously. Her friendship helped me survive a lonely, empty time of my life. When I remember much of our lives in Sterling Heights, I remember times with Linda. The job at the clinic became a life line for me, one outside of the house I shared with Danny.

Not really understanding that I was doing it, I searched for things away from home, activities and friendships that fulfilled me. I now had church friends, church attendance, and a job I loved. They could not replace a husband and a loving relationship but as long as they existed, I could keep from lingering over the knowledge that I was lonely and for the most part ignored.

It was the winter of 1975 and Michigan was hit by a blizzard. Not a snow storm, a full blown blizzard. We awoke to several feet of snow. The busy, thronging city of Sterling Heights came to a halt. Schools and businesses shut down for what appeared to be many days of digging out. Linda and I were scheduled to work that day. She called me early in the morning.

"Can you get out of your sub?"

"No," I laughed. "Nothing is moving." The neighborhood, deep in snow, was silent. Nothing moved and the blankets of firmly packed, heavy snow created an eerie acoustic.

"Well, I think I can get out," she said. "So I can come by and pick you up if you can get out to 16 Mile Road."

"Sure, I'll get my high boots on and walk out there." Linda gave me a time to be out at the highway. We were two streets into the subdivision before the highway.

"Well, I'm sure I won't be able to actually come to a stop. Nothing's been plowed so I have to keep my little car going in the tracks already made in the snow. So, you need to be out there on the side of the highway," she explained. "When you see me coming, I'll open the door, slow down as much as I can, and you hop in."

"Sounds good to me." I told her. "I'll get in my snow gear and start out right away." Danny thought I was crazy and said so, but it sounded like fun to me.

Bundled up and boots on, I headed out. The snow was packed a foot or more at the side door into the garage. I climbed up and over the mound on my way out to the sidewalk. A few people were out shoveling and snow blowers broke the stillness. I made my way down Idaho Drive, to the cross street and finally to the highway through the white mounds of snow, almost waist deep in spots.

Once at the highway, I crossed the two north lanes, the median and the two south lanes to wait for Linda at our agreed upon spot. There was no traffic to be seen or heard. I stood, watching and waited. Before long, Linda's little faded yellow car appeared in the distance. I waved my arms frantically to let her know I was there. She honked. As the car approached, Linda slowed to a crawl, but did not stop. I watched. Just feet before she reached me, the passenger door flew open. I inched my way closer to the car, jogged close to the side and when the open door was directly at me, I jumped in. I slammed the door and Linda gave the car more gas.

We both screamed and laughed the entire trip to the clinic. Not surprisingly, we were the only employees who showed up for work that day. We spent the day cancelling appointments, laughing, talking and, in general doing whatever we wanted. By the time we left for the day, a path had been made in the highways leading to and from the clinic and my house. The following day, the city had begun to return to normal activities and the clinic was open for business. Linda and I were at our posts in the office. The director of nursing came by the office.

"You know you two were the only two people insane enough to even attempt to get into work yesterday." Linda and I laughed and told her we had a great time. "Well, for your efforts, you're both getting a bonus." Not only did we have one fun day, but we got our regular pay and a bonus.

That was life knowing Linda Silver.

My job at the clinic paid for the property in Harrison, making it possible for us to move forward with our plans to move north to Harrison.

CHAPTER NINETEEN

—⚭—

We scatter seeds with careless hand, And dream we ner'er shall see them more; But for a thousand years their fruit appears In weeks that mar the land, or healthful store.

Keble

I leaned against the kitchen counter adjacent to the oblong boxy telephone attached to the wall, the receiver resting on my shoulder with my ear pressed against it, talking to a friend. The twenty-four foot cord allowed ample movement around the 12x18 foot kitchen and I took advantage of every foot, cleaning or cooking during conversations. It was years prior to the technology of a 'beep' signaling you had another caller. Instead, the caller heard the irritating busy signal, zzz-urp, zzz-urp, endlessly repeated. That was the sound repeating itself in Janet's ear.

In the middle of my conversation a stranger's voice came on the line.

"Excuse me. This is the operator. I have an emergency call from a Janet Heins. Will you accept the call?"

"Yes," I said. I heard a clicking noise and then a brief silence. My friend was disconnected.

. Janet's voice came on the line. Sobbing, she said, "My mother has cancer." In between sobs, she explained that Milly had been diagnosed with liver cancer. It was terminal.

When Milly married Bill, she moved to Clare where Bill's home was. Over the past months she had been feeling ill. Just weeks previously her illness was attributed to the flu, but when the symptoms did not improve, the doctors said it was her ulcer. She had suffered with an on again off again ulcer for many years. Both diagnoses were wrong. Ultimately, she and her husband, Bill, were told that her illness was liver cancer. It was a particularly aggressive form, with a prognosis of six months. Dan was at work and until he came home, I had no way of telling him the news. I knew how devastating this would be for my husband. I dreaded telling him. Milly had been the center of Danny's universe his entire life. The circle of his life emanated only as far as Milly allowed. And now that control was going to evaporate.

Predictably, Dan was shattered by the news. After several telephone calls, he planned an immediate trip up north to visit Milly, who remained hospitalized. I stayed home with Julie and Michael.

Over the next six months Danny made regular trips to spend as much time as possible with his mother, spending long weekends with his sisters at Milly's bedside. The cancer progressed at an alarming rate. Milly was in and out of the hospital during the first weeks. But before long the illness kept her in the hospital, bedridden. My husband's days and weeks became working during the day, evenings spent on the telephone receiving up-dates, conversing with his sisters and then traveling north to the hospital to spend long week-ends with his family.

I remained at home with Julie and Michael. Dan and I had barely a thread of connection by this time, and that fiber was strained to its limit. There was Dan and there was his mother. I understood his sadness. Within a period of two years, I had lost both my parents at a very young age. His mother's impending death put a crushing weight on Dan and I watched from my position as bystander as he struggled to cope. I had no role in his life that might threaten to upstage Milly. No other female was allowed into the intimate circle between mother and son. Her control was unshakable. As he had all his young life, Danny allowed Milly a secure place above all things and people. I could not penetrate the circle. I learned early in our relationship that neither Milly nor Danny allowed interlopers.

This was a time in our lives when this illness, this tragedy, must be dealt with as our top priority. It impacted not just Dan, but all of us; me, Julie and Michael. We needed to face this together as a married couple. I attempted to comfort him as his wife. That was not allowed to happen. Danny's comfort and confidant had been, as always, Milly. I not only understood my status as bystander, but irrationally accepted it. Past attempts on my part to alter my role proved futile. For Danny, women in his life were items to be availed of and used. His deepest relationship was dying and he faced a future alone. It both frightened and isolated him.

Several weeks passed with Dan being gone for extended periods of time. On one weekend, I asked Joe, Milly's ex-husband and Dan's father, if he would drive Julie and me up north to visit Milly, the first time since her diagnosis. I wanted Milly to spend time with her granddaughter before she died. And I wanted to see my husband.

"Yes," Joe said. "I'll take you. I want to see Milly myself." In the years following their divorce, Joe and Milly had little contact. This was an opportunity for Joe to make a last visit as well.

Joe picked us up early Saturday morning. I was anxious to see my husband and to visit with his sisters, Janet and Terry. Joe decided to take a route that was longer but went through small cities and towns. Julie and I got a history lesson as we drove the easy, unhurried route of M-46 East towards Mt. Pleasant and the hospital. St. Louis and Alma, both small towns, were where he and Milly had grown up, Joe told us. They met there, married and spent the early years of their married life in the areas. It was fun listening to his reminisces and learning things about their early lives.

On the way we stopped at a Brown's Dairy for ice cream cones. The building was old, smaller than you would expect for such popular ice cream, and had too many flavors to count. He told Julie and me that it was a place he had gone to many times as a young man. We each got large cones to eat on the way. It was warm and the ice cream melted almost as fast as we could eat it.

"Thanks, Grandpa," Julie said from the backseat. "That was really good."

"It was very good," I added. "Thanks for stopping, Joe."

"I don't know if it was good or not," he said. "I had to eat it so fast, I hardly tasted it."

Julie and I laughed for so long that Joe could not help but start laughing along with us. I still remember Joe's kindness and the fun he put in our lives that day. It was a simple trip but Joe managed to make it an adventure.

We arrived at the hospital in the early afternoon. Dan and his sisters, Terry and Janet, sat in the waiting room. After brief hellos, we all filed into Milly's private room. She was sitting up, smiling and expressed genuine pleasure at our being there. She had lost considerable weight by now and her face appeared sunken, her color gray.

After a few minutes, Dan kissed his mom and said, "Mom, Terry, Janet and I are going to get a bite to eat while you visit with Chris and Julie."

They all left the room, taking Joe along, leaving Julie and me alone with Milly. Over the next hour we talked about the mundane. Julie sat quietly next to me. At eight years old, her grasp of the meaning of cancer was vague. Julie understood that her Grandmother was gravely ill. She and I had talked about it but her young mind did not yet possess the capacity to comprehend death's finality.

"You look very pretty today, honey," Milly said. "Did your mom make your dress?"

"Yes. It's my Easter outfit." Julie stood to model the pink dotted-Swiss dress and matching coat. Easter was a week away but Julie insisted on wearing her new outfit so her Grandmother would see how she looked. Along with the dress and coat, Julie wore her new white gloves and Easter bonnet, also white. The hat set on her head, held in place with a piece of elastic under her chin, its upturned brim marked by a bow in the back and two pieces of grosgrain ribbon hanging from the bow.

"I have a new purse too." She opened the white patent purse and held it for Milly to see inside. It was empty except for one cotton hankie, starched, ironed and neatly folded.

"It's very lovely sweetheart." Milly's voice was low, even weak, but she smiled and held out her arms to Julie. They hugged.

"And," Julie said, "I got my new Easter shoes." She put forth one small foot for Milly to admire the black patent buckle shoes and white socks with lace trim around the top.

Buying Easter shoes was an event for Julie. Once a year she and I made a trip to a small shop on Gratiot Avenue. It was not a general store or department store with shoes scattered casually around, tags hanging from one heel. Select styles were carefully displayed in the front window and inside the store myriad shoe boxes lined the walls from floor to ceiling, each one tucked neatly in place, sorted by style and size. Walking into the store, we were greeted by an older gentleman.

"Good morning ladies. What can we do for you today?" The greeting was always the same as he led us to sit down in one of the comfortable padded chairs lined up in a neat row down the middle of the store.

"We're here for Easter shoes," I said.

"Well, that's good," he smiled. "And what kind are you looking for?"

"Black patent leather Buster Browns," I said. The style never changed nor did the ritual. "Let's see what size you are young lady." Julie already had her shoe off, waiting. From under one of the chairs, he pulled out his steel elongated slide marked by different shoe sizes, one end marked *Left* and the other marked *Right*. Julie stood up and put her socked foot down on the cool steel, her heel firmly pushed to the back.

"Okay," he said. Standing up he turned to the wall of shoe boxes. Against the wall a ladder on wheels went from floor to ceiling. Pulling the ladder to a new spot, he climbed up halfway, peered through the wooden ladder rungs at the boxes, selected one and came back down the ladder, shoebox in hand. Walking back to us, he flipped the lid off the box and pulled out one shoe. The black patent glistened. Kneeling down again in front of Julie, he took hold of her foot and with great ceremony slid the shiny buckled shoe on, using the shoe horn from his back pocket to ensure her heel fit properly. He did the same for her other foot, buckled each one and leaned back. "How do those feel?"

Julie smiled. "They feel good." She walked tentatively down the carpeted floor a few steps then turned and walked back to me. "I like them."

"They are very pretty. We'll take them." I paid for the shoes and we left, Julie carrying the shopping bag with her new shoes. Sometimes we capped off our excursion with a Sanders' hot fudge sundae.

As the minutes ticked away, our conversation faded. Neither Milly nor I had ever gone out of our way to spend time together in the past, and we had little to say now. Finally, I said, "I want you to know that Dan and I are going to have a son."

"Are you pregnant?"

"No, not yet," I said. "But the Lord promised me a son. So I know that it's going to happen." I smiled.

She stared at me. It was the same stare I saw each time I shared my promise. The doubtful, oftentimes pitying, looks of others had ceased to faze me. I told her the details; my prayer late one night, God's specific promise to me from His Word, and my unwavering belief that this was going to happen just as God said.

"God is so good," I told her. "Do you remember when I lost the baby and had surgery?" She nodded and said, "Yes, that was such a terrible thing for you and Danny."

"Yes it was," I said. "But something fantastic came from that."

For the next thirty minutes, I gave her my testimony, sharing how amazing God's love and grace are to all of us. She was quiet.

In the stillness, I said, "Would you like me to pray with you?" My voice was low and tentative. I had no idea of how my offer would be received. As the words left my lips, they surprised even me. This woman did not like me, in fact, she was now openly against me.

She said a quiet "Yes." I put my hand out to take hold of hers. It was soft and small in my own. Before I bowed my head and closed my eyes to pray, I saw my eight year old daughter sitting by the bed, her eyes wide, watching and listening to her grandmother and mother.

I began to pray, with no thought of what words to say or how exactly to pray. This woman was near death. I heard myself praying the sinner's prayer. Just as I had prayed at the altar, weeping, seeking forgiveness for my own sins, and for God's abundant grace, so I prayed the same prayer for Milly. I heard clearly God's plan of salvation, forgiveness and redemption in the words I prayed.

As I finished with a quiet, "Amen," I looked up and saw understanding on Milly's face.

Shortly after, Julie and I left to take a walk outdoors. We then returned to the same waiting room to sit. Before long, Dan, Joe, Terry and Janet came back. Dan and his sisters went in to Milly's bedside. Joe, Julie and I drove back to Sterling Heights.

It was only later, that I said to myself, "I led that woman to Christ."

She lived for six months and died in July. In the end, her death was a relief for her children and a mercy for her pain ravaged body. It was wrenching for them to watch her suffer. Danny, Janet and Terry, gathered into their own private circle of grief, leaving all others out. Before, during and after the funeral, the three stood aloof from spouses, friends and relatives, huddled together to cry and grieve. My husband did not seek me out, sit with me, or speak to me at the funeral or following. I was regulated to a row behind family. I sat alone, as I often did when he became son and brother. Danny's arms wrapped around his sisters, he was oblivious to anything or anyone else.

I understood the need for a family to grieve as one. She had been their mother. It was something that no one else there shared. I knew, because I was the same at each of my parent's funerals.

But for Danny, this was an indication of something much deeper. In life, Milly had been the center of his life. In her death, he drew his two siblings into a new circle. I remained outside of their sphere. That day something new began that grew to fill the void that Milly's death had created; his sisters. He became the protector, the pseudo head of all things Milly. I heard the pounding of another nail in the coffin of our already shattering, make-believe life together. Following her funeral, we did not speak of her death or his grief. We went our separate ways.

If I had been too intimidated to stand up for my rights as a wife while Milly lived, it became even more so following her death. Her memory became the stuff of legends. She was now supermom, defying all odds to overcome obstacles and prove to be the selfless, devoted mother to her three guileless children. Suddenly all memories of the intrusion into our lives by the whispered lies, intimidation, and subtle forcing Dan to make a choice between his wife and mother, were all forgotten. She became super grandmother to the grandchildren. In the retelling, Milly rose from death to sainthood. I was shadow-boxing with a myth. And getting my brains beat out.

By September, 1976 we had sold our house in Sterling Heights, packed up all our belongings and headed to Harrison for a new life.

You may think you're the baddest ass in town. But let me tell you, there's always someone that's a little tougher. And someone else tougher than him...

Dan

HARRISON, MICHIGAN

1975

CHAPTER TWENTY

An unguarded strength is a double weakness.
Oswald Chambers

Our beautiful brick ranch home in Sterling Heights sold in twelve short weeks. In September of 1975 friends and family came, and in one day, loaded a large moving van, Dan's pickup truck and the old, brown station wagon with everything we owned. By day's end we were off for parts north. Dan, driving the moving van, headed up our caravan. Michael followed in the pick-up and I brought up the rear; the station wagon loaded tight with Julie and our dog, Jasper, a black Labrador retriever. Except for having a granny atop the moving van riding in a rocking chair, we looked like a city version of the Beverly Hillbillies.

Our fifteen acres of northern serenity awaited us. There was yet to be a house built on the property. Shortly after purchasing the land, we met with a local builder to choose plans for a house; a two story saltbox design with full basement, two bedrooms upstairs and a full bath, the master bedroom downstairs with full bath, a small kitchen, dining room and living room, total square feet, 1500. We decided to have it roughed in and finish the rest ourselves. Before Danny's mother, Milly, died we had made arrangements to live with her and her then husband, Bill, for the few weeks it would take to have the shell erected. Following her death, Bill insisted we live with him as planned. He lived in Lake George, a small village west of Harrison, and twenty miles from our future home.

Once Mike was enrolled in Harrison High School and Julie in Amble Elementary, Dan and I concentrated on building the house. Quickly, it seemed, a basement was dug, poured and ready for a house. The weather cooperated by providing a warm and rain-free fall in Michigan. The shell was up, the roof on and shingled by early October. It was time for the inside to take shape. This Dan and I did ourselves. Michael worked with us each day after school and on week-ends. Dan, with some help from a reference book, did the plumbing. My contribution consisted of running for parts, picking up tubs, toilets, and sinks.

Typically, Dan made a detailed list for me to take on my journey for parts and supplies. In 1975 Home Depot and Lowe's were as yet in the future. Mt. Pleasant, an eighty mile round trip, was our closest source for necessary building needs. Dan's skills were best put to work on the actual construction rather than being spent in travel time. I was the perfect go-fer. He ordered much of what was needed over the telephone, ending with "my wife will pick it up."

There were no cell phones. Our new address did not have a house and certainly not a telephone line. The only telephone available to us was in Lake George at our temporary living quarters, a distance of twenty miles. Once Dan arrived at the work site on Wilson Road, he was incommunicado and so, after being given my assignment along with a detailed list, I went over the items until I was confident no mistakes would appear in the bounty I brought back.

"Okay, what should I ask for specifically?" List in hand, I looked to my husband.

"It's all on the list," he said. "You should be okay."

"Is there more than one choice on any of these parts or pieces of things? Is there some detail I need to know?"

"No, that's it," Dan said.

"Are they going to ask me something I won't know?" Better to be prepared was my motto.

"No, just give the list to whoever is at the counter," Dan assured me. "I talked to the guy yesterday."

It sounded simple enough and off I went to the Plumbing Supply in Mt. Pleasant. Today, I would call Dan on his cell phone from my cell phone, hand the phone to the salesman and the two would figure it out. I would even take a picture of the item in question and send it to Dan, hoping Mike was there to show Dan how to open a picture on his cell phone. But not this day.

I stood inside the Plumbing Supply store surrounded by funny looking parts I could not identity, toilets, pipes of all sizes and shapes, and men in jeans, t-shirts, work boots and baseball caps. The man behind the counter stared at me, waiting for an answer to his question of "which one do you need?"

"I don't know the answer to that, but I need this part," I pointed to the item on my list. "And I'm not leaving without it."

He stared some more.

"Look, just tell me everything you can about this thing." I could not name the strange looking curving silver piece in my hand that the salesman had suggested as what I might or might not want. "And I'll let you know when something sounds familiar to me." I leaned on the counter and waited. He talked about plumbing. I listened until the language sounded familiar.

"That's it," I stopped him in mid-sentence. "That's what my husband needs it for and what it has to do." I paid for all the items on my list, most of which looked the same, round and silver, got in the truck and headed north.

October all too quickly turned to November. The house was enclosed by now, keeping Michigan winter weather out. The plumbing was finished, and a furnace installed. The electrician was in the process of finishing the wiring. For this, he spent most of his time in the basement, out of sight. Dan remained on the main floor, taping and sanding drywall. A nasty job. The main living area had a majestic twenty foot ceiling, requiring Dan to be high on scaffolding. The result was a nasty barrage of drywall dust floating in the air, leaving a thick white film everywhere. Our goal was to move in by Thanksgiving. Much of what remained was cosmetic and we were anxious to be in the house. By mid-November each time we made a trip to the new house, we loaded up boxes, dishes, furniture, whatever fit in the available space.

It was a Saturday. The night before left inches of snow on the ground. Dan was at the house working. Mike, Julie and I loaded up the station wagon and drove to the Wilson Road house. As I turned the corner off of Old 27, a two-lane highway, onto Wilson Road, a dirt road, the rear driver's side tire went flat. After nearly thirteen weeks of living out of boxes, driving back and forth, the upheaval of construction, driving both kids to two different schools every day, and living in chaos, I was experiencing some stress. Dan may have referred to my state of mind as on the edge of insanity; maybe even one foot firmly planted in the sea of craziness. The flat tire flipped the top of the pressure cooker.

I got out of the car and without a word to Mike or Julie, walked the one-half mile to the house. By the time my shoes hit the porch, reason had fled. I thumped the door open and stomped with a full load of attitude to where Dan stood perched high atop the scaffolding. Both feet may have now become entrenched somewhere off center of reality.

"I AM SICK OF THIS! THE CAR HAS A STUPID FLAT TIRE AND I CAN'T CHANGE IT. I'M SICK OF DRIVING BACK AND FORTH AND NOW IT'S SNOWING. HOW DO YOU CHANGE A FLAT TIRE IN THE SNOW ON A DIRT ROAD? IT'S DANGEROUS. I CAN'T DRAG ALL THOSE BOXES DOWN THE ROAD. THIS IS JUST STUPID!" My rant released, and not waiting for nor allowing a reply, I turned and walked out the door, slamming it behind me.

Dan remained silent throughout. Footsteps sounded on the basement steps and the electrician appeared at the top of the stairs. "They do get excited sometimes, don't they?" He said. Dan nodded silently.

When I got back to the vehicle, Michael had changed the tire, put the flat tire in the back of the station wagon and put the tools away as well. I got in and we drove in silence the one-half mile to the house. Only as we unloaded the newest bevy of boxes, did it occur to me that my recent, and very vocal, tirade had been witnessed by the electrician. "Hmmp," I snorted under my breath, "And you better stay out of my way too buddy."

We moved into the house and continued the finishing work. The New Year began with little fanfare. The house was completed, Julie and Michael were back to school following the holiday break, and Dan was back to work full-time. He was with a Grand Rapids based company working on the expansion to the Mt. Pleasant Hospital. I was once again, what I wanted most in life, being a full-time, stay-at-home mom, wife and homemaker.

We located a Nazarene Church in Clare, twenty-three miles south from our home. The usual three times a week attendance meant three hours of back and forth travel. It was inevitable that we soon were attending just once a week, Sunday morning worship and Sunday School. And before long, Julie and I were attending services alone.

The idea of starting a business of our own began to take shape. It became a reality when the hospital expansion project neared its end. The company wanted Dan to come to Grand Rapids and work as foreman on future projects. As flattering as that was, moving was out of the question. Equally non-negotiable was making the daily drive from Harrison to Grand Rapids. And D&J Sheet Metal & Heating was born. In the early stages Dan continued to work in Mt. Pleasant finishing up the last details on the hospital project. Evenings were spent working out of a rented garage turned shop that housed the newly acquired sheet metal machinery and equipment necessary to run our fledgling business. It was not unusual for him to go directly from Mt. Pleasant to the newly acquired sheet metal shop and work late into the evening. He worked twelve to fourteen hour days and was home very little.

I was accustomed to being alone evenings and so did not speak of it. As was my firm bent, I smiled and played the perfect understanding wife. I fully supported the business venture, never doubting Dan would make a success of whatever he set out to accomplish. He was smart, hardworking and personable. People gravitated to him. It was something that Dan took for granted and used for his own ends. My mistake then, as before, was my silence, which became acquiescence. I had grown to accept my place, not as wife, but as that of a silent, invisible entity in Dan's life. Foolishly, I made no demands on his time.

CHAPTER TWENTY-ONE

---∞∞∞---

If you have an important point to make, don't be subtle or clever.
                                                    Winston Churchill

Once settled into our new home, my thoughts turned to getting pregnant. We now lived miles from physicians or medical facilities. Finding a fertility specialist became a challenge. My promise from God for a son remained as real as it had in 1971 on the night God had spoken it to me. But I began to believe that perhaps God needed my assistance. It was a time for me to step up to the plate and give God a helping hand. It would take time to research the area, get information on doctors and hope one would turn out to be a specialist in infertility. And time was a commodity I possessed in abundance.

Late one night, I awoke from a sound sleep. Restless and unable to fall asleep again, I went out to the living room to read. The feeling failed to subside. Putting my book down, I got on my knees, intending to spend time in quiet prayer. The hushed stillness of the late night wrapped around me like a soft shawl. So real was the feeling, I did not move, fearing that I would lose this sense of comfort and safety. The silence became a reverence. I was loath to move and let it escape. Slowly I bowed my head to rest my face in my hands. Then I heard it, a voice clear and forceful. One I knew was audible to me alone.

"I want you to give back to me the promise of a son I gave to you."

I will not argue the case for, nor against, hearing God speak. If someone has not experienced it and doubts its reality, no argument, however persuasive, will bring a sudden rush of understanding. If, on the other hand, someone has heard, or does hear, in the stillness of his or her own heart and deep need, then no explanation is necessary.

On that night, I heard. My heart pounded. I drew in a sharp breath but did not look to peer into the darkness for a person. I knew exactly who was doing the talking.

In response, I whispered, "No. You can't mean that, Lord. You would not be so cruel." But God did mean exactly what I heard. Silence. I wanted God to tell me this was just a test, that He never would do such a thing.

After hearing nothing but the dark, lonely silence, I whispered again, "No. I won't do it. You cannot ask such a thing of me." With that, I got up off my knees and went back to bed.

The following days were sad, my thoughts returning over and over to those words: *Give up the promise. Give up your son. Give this gift, your most precious hope, back to Me.* I remained resolute. I would not give back this astounding promise. My next argument to God was one I saw as so amazingly logical, it was sure to shake heaven. "Lord, what will people think of You, if You go back on your word?" Putting God's reputation on the line seemed an audaciously brilliant turn of events. And, one I was certain would turn the tables in my favor.

Not surprisingly, God was not impressed with my defense, nor was He moved. Over the next several days each time I knelt to pray or opened my Bible, the same words rolled across my line of vision like a banner floating behind an airplane. God was asking me to give up my promise. Give up my son, my son not yet conceived. Days passed and it seemed heaven was shut up tight. This was a request from God, not an edict, of that I was profoundly certain. But why? What possible good could come from this disappointment. On the other hand, I could and did, list all the ways in which God would be glorified by fulfilling His promise to me. My arguments, all of which I supported with unbelievable reason, brought no response from Heaven.

Time passed. I was worn out from arguing with God. Another sleepless night. Again, I got out of bed to go into the living room thinking I would read until I was sleepy. Instead, I knelt by the couch, bowed my head in prayer. A profound sadness threatened to smother me.

"Okay Lord. I give you back your promise. It's yours. I will trust you in this matter." The whispered words enveloped me with suffocating finality. That was it. Gone. I would never have a son. Ever. No harps played songs from heaven. No angels sang. It was dark outside and darker still inside my soul. No voice from heaven whispered back to me, *"That's all I wanted to hear. You get it all back as a reward."* I did not hear such words, nor did I expect to. It was final and in my world, irrevocable. I got up off my knees and went back to bed.

Weeks went by. When I thought of that night of surrender, it was accompanied by an impenetrable sense of loss. My days went on as usual. Nothing had changed outwardly. Inwardly, I mourned for what was not to be. I did not question God. I did not rage against an injustice perpetrated upon me. God was God. He remained sovereign in my life.

April came. I ceased doctor visits. There was no point. All thoughts of becoming pregnant had left my head. I did not speak of it to anyone, certainly not Dan. A part of me wanted to protect God's reputation and I thought this might make Dan think less of God. And, I reasoned, Dan already thinks I am a little crazy. He did not need further evidence.

Several weeks later, home alone, I sat down to read and turned to the Old Testament.

> *One day Elisha went to Shunem. A prominent woman of the city invited him in to eat, and afterwards, whenever he passed that way, he stopped for dinner. She said to her husband, "I'm sure this man who stops in from time to time is*

*a holy prophet. Let's make a little room for him on the roof;
we can put in a bed, a table, a chair, and a lamp, and he
will have a place to stay whenever he comes by."*

*Once when he was resting in the room he said to his servant
Gehazi, "Tell the woman I want to speak to her."*

*When she came, he said to Gehazi, "Tell her we appreciate
her kindness to us. Now ask her what we can do for her.
Does she want me to put in a good word for her to the king
or to the general of the army?"*

"No," she replied, "I am perfectly content."

"What can we do for her?" he asked Gehazi afterwards.

He suggested, "She doesn't have a son,. . ."

"Call her back again," Elisha told him.

*When she returned, he talked to her as she stood in the door-
way, "Next year at about this time, you shall have a son."*

"O man of God," she exclaimed, "don't lie to me like that."

*But it was true; the woman soon conceived and had a baby
boy the following year, just as Elisha had predicted* (II
Kings 4:8-17, TLB).

I stopped reading, not allowing my mind to go in the direction
to which my heart was racing. Despite my best efforts to hear nothing, there it was again, the voice.
"That is for you."
"No," I spoke the one emphatic word aloud. I was not going to
get on that ride again. That was April of 1976.

CHAPTER TWENTY-TWO

—❧—

Before the year was out, Hannah had conceived and given birth to a son.
She named him Samuel, explaining, "I Asked God for him."

I Samuel 1:20 (KJV)

"The tenth of May. That's the day I conceived," I said. The insurance representative listened politely.

"Can I ask how you know the exact date?" She was not convinced. More than mere skepticism, her voice told me I was borderline delusional. We were discussing technicalities in our insurance that would nullify maternity coverage as of the first of June so the date of conception was an important point.

"When you've been trying to get pregnant for ten years, you know the date when it finally happens," I said.

Just two weeks earlier I had secretly gone to a doctor to have my suspicions confirmed. This physician, a general practitioner, was a reasonable distance from Harrison. I still did not know anyone in the area well enough to ask for a recommendation and so I scanned the Yellow Pages for a physician. I wanted the pregnancy confirmed in order to surprise Dan. The test confirmed that I was pregnant. My thrill, however, was short lived.

I had just finished reciting my medical history, including the ectopic pregnancy, when the doctor abruptly said, "Well, this is another ectopic. No doubt. They always happen in both tubes." As I stared open-mouthed, he added, "You need immediate surgery to remove it."

I stopped breathing. "What? Why?" I whispered. The cold hard examining table beneath me shook as my hands grabbed its sides.

"Go home, tell your husband and call back. We will set a date for surgery right away." With that, he walked out of the examination room. His callous treatment of so devastating a statement left me in stunned silence. Terrified, my only thought was to get home to Danny. I dressed, tears rolling down my face, and left without a word to anyone.

The office was twenty-five miles from home and I sobbed every mile. This could not be happening. Once in our driveway, I sat to compose myself. Getting out of the car moments later, I stepped onto the porch and into the house.

Dan looked at my tear streaked face and said, "What's wrong? What happened?" He was looking me over to see if I was injured or bleeding. I choked out the entire story. His response was immediate and absolute, "That's bullshit. No way in hell am I letting anyone cut you open." Exhausted from crying, I made no reply. "Tomorrow we are finding a different doctor," he added. I let him hold me.

I spent the night waiting for my insides to explode as they had seven years ago. In the morning, groggy and nauseous, I sat on the couch watching my husband use the same method I had used just two days previously. Dan flipped through the Yellow Pages until he found another doctor. Doctor Coles, an OB/GYN in Mt. Pleasant, was forty miles south of Harrison. I sat, silent, while Dan made a telephone call to demand an appointment. I was frightened and thankful that my husband was now in control.

"Listen, my wife is pregnant," he said. "Some quack told her that it's an ectopic pregnancy and wants to cut her open. I want her to see someone who knows what they're doing." He paused, listening. "Okay, we can be there by then," he said and hung up the phone. "Get dressed. You have an appointment in a couple of hours." I knew he was angry but not at me. Dan had little tolerance for stupidity and less so when it caused fear or cruel treatment of his family.

Dan's easy going manner, jubilant nature and charm were admired by people who often remarked to me, "He is so calm all the time. That must be nice to live with someone like that." People rarely, if ever, saw the Dan that emerged when someone crossed his line. I had. As upset as I was with the doctor of the previous evening, I was glad, for his sake, he was not sitting before my husband right now.

"You can sit up," the nurse told me. I was shaking, but not from the chill in the small exam room. I sat up, tucked the sheet around me, and waited for Dr. Coles to speak. Realizing that I was holding my breath, I slowly let out a long sigh.

"You have a healthy, normal pregnancy," he said. "You are between six and seven weeks along. This is not, I repeat, not an ectopic pregnancy."

"Are you sure?" I began to cry, a tiny hope covered in panic. "How do you know?"

Doctor Coles visibly drew himself up to his full height and said, "Because I am an OB/GYN."

His indignation at any other time would have made me laugh. But now, hearing his arrogant, self-assured declaration was a lifeline, a link to sanity in my fear. "And because I have twenty plus years of experience," he finished as he looked at me. His egotism, which made his bedside manner less than warm and fuzzy, carried me through the next eight months. For all my fears, worries and imagined traumas, Dr. Coles remained sure of himself, and that was reflected in me.

The look on my face as I walked back into the waiting room told Dan all he needed to know. My due date, the fourteenth of February, seemed an eternity away. I should have been jubilant, rejoicing that my promise from the Lord was a reality. Instead, I was sick with anxiety. Over the next ten days, I walked around in a daze, afraid to sleep or be left alone. At night I watched the clock next to our bed, waiting for 2:00 a.m. to come and go. Only then was I able to fall asleep, the awful hour now passed.

Following my second pre-natal appointment, eleven weeks into my pregnancy, I relaxed and allowed myself to be happy. When it was time to hear the baby's heartbeat for the first time, Dan was with me, listening to the strong beat. After, the nurse casually asked, "So, are you hoping for a boy or a girl?"

"Oh, it's a boy," I said. It was 1976 and ultra-sounds were still in the future but I already knew my baby was a boy just as God had promised. "The miracle is that I am pregnant," I told her. "God promised me six years ago that I would have a son, so I know this is a boy." I smiled. Dan stared at the wall. The nurse left the room without a word. I did not care. I knew I was right.

Over the next six and a half months, awkward silence was a common reaction from people. I was never shy or hesitant in announcing that I was carrying a boy and how I knew. Dan never verbally expressed doubts, but he feared that, if our baby was a girl, I would be heartbroken. He very much wanted a son, but boy or girl, Dan was overjoyed about having another child. I secretly laughed, because I knew he was in for a big surprise.

In October, at my regular visit, the doctor talked to me about a new strain of flu that was spreading, the Swine flu. "There is a vaccine," he said. "But it hasn't been tested on pregnant women."

"So, do you recommend that I get vaccinated?"

"Well, that's entirely up to you," he said. "But I have seen pregnant women die from the flu." And as an added perk, he continued, "This vaccine has not been tested on the fetus either." Leaving the office, I drove home to get advice from Dan.

"You need to pray about it," he said. Dan was in no way following the Lord at this time in his life, but he was not stupid either. He appreciated that prayer was real and a big part of my life. He knew that I got answers from God.

"But, I will tell you this," he said, "you can get all the advice you want from all the people you want Chris; but in the end, the decision is yours to make. And just remember that whatever decision you make, when the axe falls, it falls on you." As he so often did, Dan distanced himself from me leaving me to sink or swim. However crudely given, it was advice that I have carried with me ever since.

And pray about it is exactly what I did. "Lord," I said, "I don't know what to do. Please tell me what to do." I knew that God would direct me in the best course of action for me and for my son. And just as my promise for this son I was now carrying had come from the Word of God, so did my answer.

In the Book of Daniel, Daniel and his companions were taken to Babylon, and while in captivity were given food and wine from the King's table. Daniel refused to eat the rich foods or drink the wine, explaining to the chief official that to do so would be defilement for them. As Jews, they were obedient to the Mosiac Laws regarding diet. Instead, Daniel asked that they be given water and vegetables only for a period of ten days to show that in this way, he and his companions would flourish. And flourish they did, because they trusted in God. That was what I decided to do.

I refused the flu shot and ceased to have any concern over the flu or any other aliment. Like Daniel and his companions in the king's palace, I remained healthy and energetic throughout the pregnancy. My due date was approaching and I was anticipating announcing to family and friends the arrival of our son. His name, Samuel, was a foregone conclusion; we needed only to add a middle name and decided on Samuel David. It had a beautiful sound to it. Dan thought we should have a girl's name, just in case, but I told him it was unnecessary. I was having a boy.

I decided to have the birth announcements printed up before Samuel David made his arrival. "I have all the information I want on the announcements," I told the clerk at the newspaper office, "but I will have to call you from the hospital with the exact date, time, and weight."

She looked down at the slip of paper. "You already have the name on it," she said. "How do you know it's a boy?"

"The Lord promised me a son several years ago," I told her. "This is him." I smiled. Her expression told me she thought I was nuts.

Early in the morning of January thirty-first, I sat on the floor of our small bathroom, Big Ben in front of me, timing contractions. At 5:00 a.m., I whispered to Dan, "I think we need to go to the hospital." He told Michael we were leaving but let Julie sleep.

On the drive to the hospital, Dan stopped at the Whitehouse, an all-night restaurant in Clare, for a cup of coffee to go. "My wife's in labor and we're on our way to the hospital," he told the waitress. She looked out at the car, saw me sitting in the front seat, and then to Dan again. He smiled, took his coffee and we drove to Mt. Pleasant.

When Samuel David made his appearance on January 31, 1977 at 12:08 p.m., my husband was with me in the delivery room. At my final push, Dan said to me, "It's a boy!" My exhausted reply was, "I know."

Not for one moment from the time the pregnancy was confirmed, did I doubt that the child I carried was a boy. I called the same clerk at the newspaper office later that day with the added information for the birth announcements. Her quiet "Wow" made me smile. Dan made numerous telephone calls with the news. Family and friends expressed much the same sentiment, "Wow."

In the years to follow, the faith that carried me through that time, confirming in me that God is sovereign, real and means what He says, kept me sane as my world fell apart and every fragile thing in our lives was attacked almost to annihilation.

CHAPTER TWENTY-THREE

---⊗⊗⊗---

Is it not penetrating to realize that God knows where we live and the
kennels we crawl into.

Oswald Chambers

It was the 1980s and Michigan, according to many, was in danger of becoming a ghost town as men and women left in droves seeking work elsewhere. In Northern Michigan the recession we had only read about was fast becoming a reality. Our new business, D&J Sheet Metal & Heating, just three years old, struggled under the strain of the faltering economy. We were not alone. Small businesses everywhere around us strained to stay afloat hoping to wait out the lean times. For many individuals, the answer was to leave the state and look for greener pastures. We did not consider that an option. But still, there were bills to pay, groceries to buy and a home to maintain.

My sister's husband, Lowery, worked as an independent welder in the flourishing oil fields. The work was plentiful, and the hours long, demanding and exhausting. Lowery offered Dan a job in the fields working with him as a welder's helper. It was mind-numbing labor and paid little. But it was a paycheck. Providing for his family was Dan's foremost priority. In this, he never faltered. To not work, because he did not like the job was not merely foreign to Dan, it was inconceivable.

I went in search of employment as well. As I had done in the past when job hunting, I searched want ads. There was little to choose from in the local papers. I was not adverse to driving around the different areas and inquiring at local businesses. It was still not something I enjoyed or was comfortable doing, but as I had done in the past, I put on my confident face and made face-to-face inquiries. I happened upon a new medical clinic opening in Houghton Lake, just twelve miles north of us. I applied and because of my previous experience in a doctor's office, was hired as a receptionist. I was no more thrilled to be working in this doctor's office than I had been the first time in Sterling Heights. The pay was less than Dan's but the job carried other benefits; full family medical insurance and free unlimited medical care at the clinic from all the doctors. That proved valuable. Samuel, now almost four years old, was proving to be fearless. His head alone was the reason for three trips to the clinic for x-rays and stitches.

Despite the benefits, the job was mindless, boring work that devoured my days for little reward and robbed me of being with, and caring for, my young son and daughter. Dan and I spent little time together but that was not unusual. Long ago, we settled into living independent lives. It was not uncommon for days to pass with few words exchanged between us, all of which failed to rise to the level of *conversation*. On the few occasions when we did speak, it was a game of darts; short, to the point, hit your target and move on.

Dan: Are you working today? Chris: Yes.

Chris: What time will you be home? Dan: I don't know.

Dan: Did you go to the bank? Chris: Yes.

Our brief, pathetic exchanges were the depth of our passion and intimacy. Day after day, we grappled with a growing quagmire of misery, gagging on sludge but walking with mouths wide open. My loneliness was by now, an unkind friend, cloaking me, keeping me prisoner. I saw no escape.

Dan, gasping for air in a swamp of discouragement, was frantic to find ways to stop the voices inside his head that screamed at him his failure as a man. His business, despite hard work and determination, failed to prosper. He spent long hours each day in a hole of near servitude. His role of breadwinner was, to him, a dismal failure. He struggled to provide for his children, needing help from me to accomplish the most basic of provision and keep us out of debt. His spirit was in the bottom of a cesspool. Finding solace from me was not an option. To do so meant opening up a secret place in his soul that was off limits, not just to me, but to himself.

Dan pursued the options he had always sought; escape from what was real, to a fantasy of liquor, partying with buddies and, his old stand-by, women. He reached out and took hold of the familiar door, hoping that this time he would find solace. It was the door to a hell that was only too eager to welcome him back to a new level, one with room for me.

Adultery by its definition is an escape from reality. It is a chance to, for a brief time, live in a world of fantasy. The lies required to build this fortress are what make it exciting but it is a straw man without hope; instead it is a desperate pretense. This woman was unconnected from the life he lived but could not face. He walked into a fantasy with no ties and no responsibilities. This made-up world of false promises faded as quickly as the tail lights of his pick-up leaving her driveway late into the night, helping him remain outside himself and away from me, a reminder of marriage, responsibility, and commitment. Its allure was the hoax of romance, desperate lovers in the night, each speaking the dialogue of adultery. The carefully practiced script hides truth and highlights the fraud. Deception and danger are the drugs that fuel the monster. In this sham life responsibility and expectation do not exist. He could not fail in this made-up world he himself created. It was possible to continue to re-write the script for a better ending—each day and night.

Dan could not re-write me. Instead, he worked to cross me out with giant red words of EDIT. The harder the stroke of his pen, the deeper I dug in. Every ounce of my energy turned to my children and God. Almost unknowingly, Dan and I had severed all ties to each other. I walked each day on a tightrope of fear. I retreated into a world of my own, crying in secret, lying to my friends and hating myself for the coward I had become. God alone remained my comfort, my friend, and my protector.

Danny pursued what he believed to be his new life with a vengeance, his energy, thoughts and time remained focused on one thing. As the days went on, I lived life as a single mother, working and taking care of my home and children. Dan was gone. My response was, as it had always been, silence. I accepted his absences, not questioning, regardless of how long and how many days in a row he was gone twelve to eighteen hours at a time. The only differences between me and the women I saw around me living as single mothers were; I did not need public assistance and I actually had a husband. Dan's presence was peripheral, coming and going according to his own time, interest and wants. This arrangement had become firmly established over the course of our married life, and neither he nor I questioned the by now familiar pattern unfolding.

As the days turned to weeks and weeks to months, I accepted his absence from my life. People stopped asking *where's Dan*. When close friends asked, *is everything okay with you and Dan*, I lied. To survive, I saw myself as the long-suffering, patient, understanding wife. But occasionally something came along that propelled me out of my complacency.

I heard the key turn in the front door lock. The clock said 4:00 a.m. I got out of bed where I had been lying awake all night and followed Dan to the kitchen. He was opening the refrigerator.

"Where have you been?"

"I told you I had a job to look at west of Harrison," he said.

"Until 4:00 a.m.?"

"Yes," he said. "We just sat and talked, and then we went to the Swiss Inn for a beer." Dan kept his head down and concentrated on the sandwich he was making.

I said, "The bar closes at 2 o'clock. Where have you been since then?"

When he had no answers for my questions, Dan became angry. "Look, I told you where I was," almost shouting. "Then I stopped for a.hamburger."

"Then why are you making a sandwich?" He mumbled something I did not understand. I wanted to demand that he tell me the truth but I knew that would not happen, short of torture. Even then, his skill of hiding the truth was enviable. He had missed his true calling. Dan possessed the skills necessary to be an unconquerable spy.

Something snapped in me this time. Glancing down I saw the knife he used to cut the sandwich meat. I grabbed it, swung my arm up and sliced downward, aiming for his arm. The knife hit leather and stopped. *Damn*, I thought. I threw the knife down on the counter, turned and went back to bed. Incomprehensibly, neither of us spoke of the incident again.

Time passed. I was more lonely and alone than I imagined possible. Dan's guilt drove him to greater heights of contempt for me. I ignored the buzz saw screaming in my ear hoping someone else would turn off the switch in time. By this time, I was adept at swimming with sharks and believed if I continued to ignore the fins circling me, they just might swim away. I ran. I searched for an outlet, something that would make me feel good about myself.

MidMichigan Community College was located in Harrison and because it was a community college, much less costly to attend. I had no idea where a college degree might take me, nor did I think that far ahead. I loved learning. Julie was away at school and Sam was in school all day, giving me the time to concentrate on learning. Dan was a non-entity. He was not home often and when he was, as long as I did not make any demands on his time, attention or emotional energy, he did not care whether I went to school or not. This new focus kept me out of his hair, and his other very private life. It also kept me oblivious of the destruction that lay ahead. My ignorance was self-imposed.

CHAPTER TWENTY-FOUR

The problem is not the problem; the problem is your attitude about the problem. Captain Jack Sparrow

What was I doing sitting in a classroom with twenty-five strangers. It was day one of my college career. Two weeks ago I had met with an advisor, who recommended that I sign up for a full load of classes, twelve credit hours. I refused her suggestion and instead agreed to three classes. I intended to test the waters and find out whether or not I was college capable. With my sense of worth and talent at a new low, I intended to quietly and unobtrusively give college a test run.

Driving into the parking lot on day one, I parked, turned off the engine and sat staring at the large building. My hands maintained a firm grip on the steering wheel. I looked at the brand new backpack filled with books and notebooks on the seat next to me. I dropped my head down onto the steering wheel and wondered for the thousandth time what was I doing. "Look, just get out of the car and go into the building," I said. My words did little to calm the terror I was experiencing.

After several more, *I can do this* self-instructions, I got out of my car, walked across the parking lot and went inside. Gripping my sweat-wrinkled class schedule, I headed to the first class on my list. Using one of my best self-defense techniques, I smiled my engaging smile, the one I reserved for emergencies, and said a firm hello to everyone I passed in the hallway. Biting back the urge to whimper like a lost puppy, I occasionally peered down at my list for the room numbers. As I neared the end of a long hallway, my destination appeared. I followed several other students inside.

The room was crowded with young students. I headed to the back, espied an empty seat and sat down. "Hi, I'm Chris Pechacek," I said to the girl next to me. She smiled, introduced herself and immediately turned back to the equally baby-faced person on her other side. Gazing around the room, I saw a sea of cherubic faces, fresh out of high school, the ink on their diplomas still wet. I was thirty-nine years old, eighteen years out of high school. I resisted the impulse to get up, leave the building, get in my car and drive home. So far, I was exhibiting astounding bravery, but my face ached from smiling. Then the instructor walked in. My smile faded. He looked as young as the students.

"I'm going to go over my class list first," he said. "Some of you may not be on my list yet. Or, you may have wandered into the wrong class or section." My jaw clenched. I did not care whether I was on his list or not, I was not getting up in front of all these *kids* and walking out. My name was on the list. I survived the first great hurdle. The instructor explained the outline of the course, an entry level English class, as he passed around a *syllabus*, a word I had never heard before.

The rest of my first day of college went as expected, introductions in each class, helping the instructor pronounce my name, Pee-ah-check, and stuffing hand-outs into my brand new college-type backpack. My schedule was a Monday-Wednesday-Friday spread with each day ending by mid-afternoon. It had been meticulously planned to ensure I would be home before the bus brought Samuel home after school. Day one under my belt, I relaxed.

Homework consisted of endless pages of reading and a paper to write for the English class. While that was very college-like and

I enjoyed the sound of it on my tongue, it nevertheless brought a lurching panic. The next day after Dan was gone and Samuel was at school, I sat down at my brand new blue electric typewriter to write my first college assignment. Money was the subject with no other details other than *write about money*. I stared at the clean white sheet of paper properly inserted and ready for the first key-stroke. No sudden flash of creativity came to mind. I picked up the telephone to call my college freshman daughter. Julie had just weeks before moved into her dorm at Central Michigan University.

"Hi mom," Julie's voice answered on the first ring. "What's up?"

"I have a paper to write and I'm not sure how to go about it," I said. I could hear laughter in the background. Julie was living in Troutman Hall, sharing a room with three other females.

"Okay, what's the topic?" With one semester under her belt, Julie was to me an expert in all things academic. I described the topic. "Hmm, well, do you have any ideas yet?"

"Not really."

"How long does it have to be?" she asked. I explained to her that it had to be one whole 8x11 sheet, typewritten, double spaced and was due in just three days. "Are you kidding me, mom?" After her laughter subsided, she turned to her friends and said, "Hey, guys get this. My mother has a one-page paper to write and it's not due for three days." The room erupted in more laughter. Composing herself, Julie said, "Mom, what is the problem? One page and you have three days to write it?"

Before long, I realized that as a non-traditional student, which was a politically correct way of saying *old lady*, assignment dead-lines were hard and fast, required advanced planning and meant that on the due date, a paper was handed in to the instructor. For my daughter and her peers, a due date was a suggestion and always negotiable. Additionally, each assignment was weighed on their own personal scale as to importance and grade impact. If found wanting or the number of points towards a final grade ranked too low, the assignment was simply not done. I wrote my first college paper without help from my daughter or her friends.

My two years at the community college came and went. I began to view myself as a seasoned college student, capable and astute. I applied to, and was accepted at, Central Michigan University followed by a letter instructing me to attend orientation day, one specifically arranged for non-traditional students. At forty-one years old, that was me. I did not want to attend the orientation for the same reasons I avoided any new situations; they terrified me. And this proved to be the mother of all horrific, unknowable situations.

My orientation day group consisted of twenty eighteen year olds. Our first order of business was a tour of the various dorms. Next, was a detailed account of how to get into the dorm after all the doors are secured for the night should you accidentally be locked out. Drifting in and out of coherency, I tried to visualize any possible scenario that would make this bit of information useful to me. Nothing came to mind. Finally, we were introduced to the dorm resident, a capable and wise counselor should the need arise.

"Well, that wraps up the working part of your orientation." Our group leader led us outside. "But, we've got some fun things planned for you as well." Groups of people were gathering on the grass in front of the dorms. "We encourage you to stay and get involved. Having fun is the best way to get to know people."

I stood rock still and glowered at our fearless leader. My smile was gone, taken over by my Creature from the Black Lagoon stare. It was powerful and used only in the grimmest of circumstances. This was one of those times. The young woman glanced over my way and her countenance went from cruise-director-cheerleader to prey-facing-predator.

"But, if you just want to leave, that's fine too," the words came out in a rush.

I left. Julie and I had arranged to meet at the Student Union, a gathering place for students. I wanted Julie to walk me around campus and show me the buildings where my classes would begin the next week.

"Mom," Julie said when she saw me, "get rid of the purse." My purse hung from one shoulder and my backpack from the other. I looked from one to the other and back to Julie. "Mother, you can't carry a purse *and* a backpack." I stopped and quickly put my purse inside my backpack, thankful that any future embarrassment had been alleviated by my daughter's quick eye.

My day ended with having my picture taken for my student identification card, picking up my class schedule and buying textbooks at the student bookstore, which I now called the SBX along with my other university classmates. I drove home admiring the picture on my new CMU Student ID card.

Pursuing and achieving a bachelor's degree followed by a master's degree had not been in my plans. The completion took a total of five years and I graduated from both with honors. The five years gave me a focus, a plan, and a confidence sadly missing in my life. In the beginning, the goal seemed a lifetime away and, at times, an impossible dream. Neither of which were true. One thing remained; pursuing my education kept me busy and out of Dan's life. I ceased being a bothersome wife, asking too many questions, or demanding attention he had neither the time nor interest in affording me.

Repeating the fact that Dan and I lived two separate lives seems redundant. What was not seen by outsiders and even less obvious to friends and family, was that the two people living inside our home were shadows. We pretended and played our roles well. Each of us participated in the façade that had become our lives. I had succeeded in sealing away any thoughts of being a happily married woman, of being cherished and loved, desired or of even being acknowledged in his presence. We passed one another like planets in orbit; keeping to our own path, never touching or infringing on the other. We each feared crashing and burning should the slightest divergence occur. Days and weeks went by and we seldom saw one another except in passing. I forgot what it was to feel his lips on mine, his arms around me, or his voice speaking words of affection. It was a painful, treacherous life for both of us. We were a house of cards about to topple. Nothing of what we had known, or pretended to know, would survive.

CHAPTER TWENTY-FIVE

———⊶⊷———

Lies are like cockroaches. If you see one, you know there are others.
                                                            Nelson DeMille

"Who were you talking to on the pay phone?" I said. Dan stood next to his truck. Moments earlier I drove past the convenience store a short distance from our house and saw my husband talking on the pay telephone outside the store.

"What the hell are you talking about?" He shouted.

"Who were you talking to that you couldn't talk from here, at home?" Stopping at a public telephone just short of home raised questions I knew I could no longer ignore. The caverns of lies and deception Dan had created began to crack. A torrent of unimaginable pain was beginning to sweep over me, savage and unstoppable. His angry response was not new. It was his prescribed reaction to any crack in the armor of secrets he wore so easily. The deeper the lie, the more vicious the response to any hint of suspicion on my part. It had worked for all the years of our married life. Any questions were met with resentment. Unable to defend his secret life, he dared not let it be opened up to light. Lying and then not talking about the lies or having his lies questioned, was his primary defense.

"I don't know what you're talking about," he said.

"Yes, you do."

I followed him into the pole barn and waited for an answer. I knew the encounter would be ugly. My stomach churned. I held my hands into fists at my side to keep from shaking. I hated conflict. Any hint at raised voices, features contorted with anger, brought a familiar panic. The muscles in my legs tightened to keep me from running someplace to hide.

And this time, I had reason to be fearful.

His face, contorted with anger, stared at me in the confines of the pole barn. He was guilty. To what extent, I had yet to understand. The brown eyes stared intently into my own, daring me to question his authority. This response had never failed to silence me. Fearing his anger, I dared not pursue a truth I was terrified to face and incapable of processing. I was defenseless, devoid of any tools with which to cope in the abyss I knew awaited me as the reality of my life began to crumble.

"Who were you talking to?" The scene was unfolding just as each encounter of the past. Dan was guilty. The truth stood between us, taunting, like a snake charmer, threatening to let loose the viper.

"I had to call someone about a job," he said. "So what?" Turning his back to me, he began putting away tools and unloading his truck. "Can't I take care of business?" I was being dismissed.

"Why didn't you just call from here?" I said. "Who is it that you can't talk from home?" I knew the answer.

Backed into a corner, he turned to me, "Look, I don't want to talk about this now." There it was. A crack in the wall. A tiny tear in the carefully formed web and it was about to unravel.

"You were calling a woman," I said. "Who is she?" I did not want to hear his answer. There was nowhere for me to run and hide. There was no place to go. We stared at each other.

Finally he looked at me and said, "Yes." I stopped breathing. My heart pounded, echoing in my ears. All rational thought disappeared. I went from fear to anger to panic to rage in seconds. If it is possible to have an out of body experience, this was it. Time seemed to freeze.

"Are you going to leave me?" I whispered. The words were out before I could stop them. I did not want to hear the answer. Logic told me to throw him out. He deserved this whore. They deserved each other. But logic was as far from my thinking at that moment as the east is from the west. Suddenly, so many things made sense. The stories and long absences jarred into focus.

"No," he said. Rather than assure me, his arrogant tone made me angry. This was going to be a long road in a tortuous journey. I wondered if it would ever end. And I questioned if I could survive. I wanted to hurt him in a very real way. But I was terrified to show anger. My throat constricted. I waited. This could not be happening. My world stopped. If a semi had suddenly stopped on top of my chest, shifted gears and popped the clutch, this is what it would feel like.

"Look, it's over," he said. "I don't want to talk about it." Again, the arrogant tone, no shame or sorrow. A litany of thoughts raced through me, most of which involved Dan on the ground at my feet, and me reloading a pistol. Such feelings remained silent for the moment, but I was stepping into a chasm of emotions I did not know existed that would unleash in me things that, until that moment, seemed unimaginable. I became someone I did not know. I discovered an entire set of words I was not aware I had heard before, certainly not spoken.

I turned away from him, left the pole barn and walked alone to the house. Satan was now presenting his bill and expected payment in full. We, Dan's family, were the gratuity on this bill.

The days ahead became surreal. I stopped eating. I lost twenty-five pounds in three weeks. I did not sleep. My life was a lie. Until now, the lies I told myself had sufficed; allowing me to sleep in a world of make-believe, but his words, once uttered could not be unsaid. The fragile pieces of the life I imagined and so desperately sought to protect and nurture, cracked and fell to the ground. The shattering sound tore into my soul. At times I questioned my sanity.

I waited for the pain to go away. It did not. Daily, and without warning, panic gripped me. Unbidden, my body shook uncontrollably; tears flowed, leaving me exhausted. I had nowhere to go for comfort. Self-recriminations screamed inside my head. *How stupid can one person be? What an idiot. You are so worthless. This is what happens when you love someone, when you believe them and trust them. Stupid.* But most sinister of all the accusing voices was the one that cried out to me, *coward*.

The following weeks I went from crazy to desperate to angry and back again. Dan's aloof arrogant attitude did little to reassure me. He did not display sorrow or admit guilt. He did not ask my forgiveness. He made no attempt to reassure me in any way, but instead, treated me with a wounded tolerance. I felt his pity and contempt.

Finally, in a desperate attempt to make my hurt go away, I made an appointment with a counselor. A part of me fought for a fix, a magic potion that would sooth and heal my wounds. I found one in the Yellow Pages. My memory failed to remind me of how that had not worked the last time I applied it.

Sitting in front of this counselor, I stared in stunned silence as he told me I needed to be a better wife. The guilt engulfed me. This was all entirely my fault, according to the PhD behind the desk. His words were preposterous, of course. But to my panic-riddled mind, they made sense. This PhD went on to give me his sage advice on how to be a better wife. *Cook for him, tell him you love him, and do not bring up the painful past. Your husband wants to get beyond it now. Nothing will be gained by bringing it up. You have to just bury it.* Even in my pain-numbed state I thought about burying this man instead.

Leaving his office, I whispered, "Asshole. What a prick." Despite my disdain for this man, and the horrible lies he uttered, his words echoed in my head. By the time I arrived back home, my desperation had convinced me that maybe it was all me. Over the next weeks, I smiled, cooed, cooked, cleaned, did yard work and absorbed my pain back into what was left of my soul. Day after day I stuffed down the tears and torment. I clenched my teeth to hold back my anger, fearful that Dan would walk out should I dare to speak. I played the role of a perfect, non-complaining wife, ready to jump at the master's command. I silently stuffed down every feeling and emotion attempting to rear its ugly head. I read my Bible and prayed, desperate for a remedy to the decay eating me alive. Days turned to weeks. But nothing stays buried forever.

"God!" I screamed to heaven. "I've done everything I'm supposed to do, and this is what I get?" Like someone blowing a balloon bigger and bigger, hoping it will finally float high into the sky and disappear, I blew until my lungs refused to expand. But I did not float away from the reality smothering me.

"God, how dare you let this happen to me?" I argued with God that living a faithful life was a waste, maybe I should become what I so despised, and what I knew my husband disdained and held in contempt. Even as the words left my mouth, I knew it was not possible. The idea of becoming an unfaithful wife out of revenge was unfathomable to me. I could not.

Late one evening and home alone, I poured a glass of wine into one of my delicate pieces of crystal stemware. Too edgy to sit, I paced back and forth in our family room. The pounding in my chest and the knots in my stomach clawed their way up my throat, choking me. Tears running down my face, an ominous growl traveled up from some strange place deep within, erupting in a primal scream. The crystal flew against the paneled wall, and wine ran down to the floor. Stunned for a moment, I stood motionless, staring at the shattered crystal and pool of wine now in the carpet.

I was surprised at the sudden release I experienced. It felt so good that I went to the cupboard, took down the remaining stemware, lined them up, poured wine into each smoky glass and repeated the process until only one of my once treasured goblets remained. This rage so sudden in its eruption, so dark in its ferocity and so virulent in its thirst for revenge, that for a brief moment, it frightened me. But I also felt powerless to stop its explosion. And then, coming from someplace deep and dark, a stream of curse words erupted. Every profanity I had ever heard, read, thought about or imagined, and a few unknown to my own ears rolled off my tongue like oil on a hot pan, spitting and popping, searching for something to burn. The tirade went on, unstoppable. My throat ached and my hands hurt from clenching my fists.

And then it was over.

I dropped to the couch, my legs shaking. Taking deep breaths, my heart rate slowed to normal. I felt relaxed for the first time in weeks. The wall was covered with the remnants of wine that led to a pile of broken glass on the carpet. For the next hour, I swept and vacuumed, stooped over to carefully pick tiny pieces of the delicate crystal out of the dense carpet, and mopped up wine. Finished, I stood back and smiled. My calm satisfaction was further enhanced by gulping wine from each glass before sending it and its contents hurtling across the expanse of the family room.

The respite was just one step on a road too long to contemplate traveling but still dragged me kicking and screaming onto its hot, rocky path.

CHAPTER TWENTY-SIX

Sometimes you just have to close your eyes, count to ten, take a deep breath, remind yourself that you wouldn't look good in prison stripes and just smile at that dumb ass and walk away.

Anonymous

I pushed my grocery cart down one aisle after another, automatically reaching for items on the shelves. And then, I saw her. In my grocery store. In my town. The familiar blind rage that resulted in all my broken crystal took over. My first thought was to ram this cart into her, knock her ugly ass down and then run the wheels over her face.

I did not do that. Instead, I calmly opened my purse, got a nickel out of my wallet, walked up to her cart as she examined the packages of hamburger in the meat counter and waited until she noticed my presence.

"Hello, whore," I said. She stared at me but made no reply. I took the nickel in my hand, flipped it into her grocery cart, and said, "This ought to cover services rendered."

She left the cart full of groceries, with the nickel, and turned to leave. I followed her, my own cart of groceries left behind. She sped towards the door. I walked faster. At the main door, I watched as she got into her car.

"Oh no you don't, bitch," I whispered. In a dead run, I got to my own car as she drove out of the parking lot. Jumping into the drivers' seat, I started my car and followed her. I had no idea what I was going to do should I overtake her in a hot pursuit, but the chase made me feel good. And my fervent hope was that this woman was genuinely frightened of me. It was little comfort, but still, it brightened my day.

After two or three turns, I lost sight of her car. Given that we were in downtown Harrison, which consists of one short main street, it seemed odd that the chase was short-lived and unsuccessful. And now, sitting in my car, staring at the empty street, it occurred to me that I had given no thought as to what I would do beyond following her vehicle. I drove home. Without my groceries.

I could not undo what had happened. I had no control over the acts of others but doing something gave me a sense of accomplishment and power that had never been a reality for me in the past. I decided to go to her house and confront this woman. Dan told me her name, where she lived, and her telephone number. Once finished, he moved on, shedding her like old work clothes.

The two met during a furnace installation months previously. And Dan signed up to continue installing. In anticipation of greener pastures, and with encouragement from my husband, this woman got rid of her husband in hopes of trading hers for mine. With the ink not dry on her divorce papers, the two began their tryst. She had four children, no job, no skills, and needed another provider. As the weeks passed with Dan showing no signs of leaving me to move in with her, she grew impatient. The reality of life broke through the haze of the illusion they each had created. Winter was approaching, her bills were piling up and she needed a man with a steady income. She gave Dan an ultimatum, leave your wife and children, move in with me, or be replaced by someone else. In this, she over-estimated her charm. She, like the women before her, was a diversion, an escape that once played out, held no value. Expert at playing this game, he knew who, and what she was; for sale to the highest bidder. Dan had already left the auction.

I drove the miles south to the house, pulled into her driveway and sat staring at the farmhouse, barns, and silent windmill, its blades unmoving. The large yard was unkempt, almost wild looking. The heavy branches of an enormous tree directly in front of the house were in desperate need of trimming. Smaller limbs coming off the larger trunk hung low blocking several windows. The house, a two-story asbestos-sided saltbox design, showed its age and obvious neglect. Apparently, her plans for Dan included more than his skills in the bedroom.

An old blue station wagon was parked close to the house. I got out of my car and walked around to the back of the house. Three small wooden steps led to the wooden screen door. There was no porch. I stood on the narrow piece of worn lumber at the door. This love nest was going to keep Dan busy and broke for a long time to come. I laughed. This person, whatever she was, did not know Dan. But, I doubted that pillow talk, if they talked at all, included a *honey-do-list*. That would be a fantasy-romance killer.

"Hello," I hollered. No one came to the door or answered my call. I was not surprised by the silence. Had I been the other woman hiding somewhere back inside the house, I would have kept quiet and stayed put. Standing on the steps afforded me a clear view into the kitchen and beyond to a hallway, and what I assumed was a living room. I called out, louder this time. Again, no answer. I waited. Inside, next to the door was a mat for shoes and boots. Setting on the mat, neatly lined up next to a pair of women's shoes, set a pair of men's boots, large, brown well-worn boots. I smiled. *Well, well, you didn't waste any time in replacing one for another. The spare has arrived.*

I drove home, angry that my effort to confront this woman had been denied by her cowardice. Although obviously adept at lying, sneaking in dark holes, and stealing, she seemed not too strong in standing up for a grand passion.

Weeks passed. If I had expected the pain to disappear, I was wrong. Daily, sometimes hourly, recollections and bright lights of clarity about past unexplained events screamed in my head. I was angry with no place to spill out the bile whirling inside of me. The few friends in whom I had confided offered the same advice: *leave.* And when I did not immediately pack my belongings and run, their sympathy went to feigned pity, then disbelief, and finally, avoidance. I understood their incredulity. Others suggested books on forgiveness. I read the books. I did the exercises the authors promoted as a promised fix-it to whatever ails you. I found a book on self-hypnosis. I could not make sense of that idea. I wondered who, if I hypnotized myself, was going to give me the promised instructions for freedom in my mind. And then, who would bring me out of hypnosis, I wondered.

Another recommended author suggested it was necessary to re-train your brain and blot out old memories. My years of distance running had produced in me the value of training. I reasoned that if I could discipline my body to the rigors of running, it would work on my brain as well. For several nights I went to sleep, ear-phones firmly in place to listen to the author's positive thinking CDs while I slept. My brain must have slept as well, because nothing of what he droned on about came to mind during my days. I read an article on aroma therapy. The author postulated that the scent of lavender had the ability to heal damaged emotions and ward off depression. I bought lavender oil and slathered my wrists, ear lobes, and neck. I added lavender in a spray, covering my pillow and sheets. The sickly, sweet smell failed to produce what I had hoped. I just smelled purple.

A few friends invited me to seminars on the power of positive thinking. And when the newest and brightest failed to yield the purging I sought, I blamed myself. I walked trapped in a strait-jacket of grief. The days dragged, my feet sinking into a quicksand of anger and sorrow. The harder I tried to escape, the deeper I sank. I was alone in this hellhole.

"You need to attend this healing retreat." A friend was convinced that if I participated in the ritual of healing past hurts and memories, my grief would be over, vanished into thin air. I was willing to try anything, however ethereal, that promised an escape from what my life had become.

"What happens when I get to the retreat?" I was willing but wary.

"Someone will take you through steps of releasing each hurt, past and present," she said.

"And…?" I waited for the punch line

"Once you walk the steps of healing, you can be free. They are released once and for all," she said. Her confident smile did nothing to reassure me.

"Right." I declined her offer.

Another friend offered advice I am convinced came from a bumper sticker or kitchen refrigerator magnet. "You can't change the past so you simply have to let it go."

My immediate reaction to her well-meaning but ill-advised comment was to stare fixedly in her direction and bite the sides of my mouth to keep silent the refrain forming in my mind. Giving my friend a four letter directive on what she might do to herself seemed overly harsh given that she was trying to be helpful.

What I did not do, the one thing I denied myself, was speaking up and expressing my anger to the person I was most angry with, Dan. I silently fought this battle alone. This was an ill-advised strategy.

CHAPTER TWENTY-SEVEN

———⊗⊗⊗———

Get up offa that thing,
and dance 'till you feel better,
Get up offa that thing,
and dance 'till you sing it now!
Get up offa that thing,
and dance 'till you feel better,
Get up offa that thing,
and try to release that pressure!
Get up offa that thing,

James Brown

"Let me go." I said the words daily to a God I believed had betrayed me and left me abandoned in a cesspool of hurt. I pleaded to be free from my heartache and pain. "This is too hard," I cried. "I cannot do this." Sick with hurt, I ran blindly to escape the darkness of my grief. Days turned to weeks, and weeks to months as I grieved for the life I had pretended was real but never existed. Self-contempt ballooned around me. I berated my innocence. I was in free fall, alone, heading to the bottom and praying the crash would be merciful and quick.

My husband's adulteries put me in a chain gang. Day after day I marched shackled to something I was convinced controlled me. I saw no option but to keep in step with the taskmaster pulling me along against my will. The scenery never changed. I walked locked in a line for which I believed I had no key, pulled along by the cruel actions of others.

Forgetting is impossible. Pretending it never happened is beyond comprehension. Expecting to simply *get over it* is ludicrous. You do not get over a grief that swallows your soul and mocks your faithfulness. I believed that I would never outrun this grief; it followed me day and night, whispering in my ear, reminding me, cajoling me with its cunning like a monster that will not die or fade away. This grief would be something I would always wear, its talons burrowed into the secret part of my soul like a pox, hot and ready at a moment's notice to burst open once again. However much I tried to deny its rule over me, I remained powerless to walk beyond its reach.

And then one day, I stopped running. Standing still, my feet planted in territory of my own, I turned around and shook hands with this grief. We are becoming acquainted. I have developed a profound respect for this grief and marvel at what I have learned and continue to learn from our collaboration.

An innocence is gone; slain and buried in the depth of the dark waters where the Creature of the Black lagoon lives. While I mourn for that person, I am not angry at her. She did a good thing; loved passionately and faithfully, expecting good in return. That is never a bad thing. I respect her for her strength in the face of chaos. I admire her courage. I marvel at her tenacity in doing what was right and good in the midst of the storms.

This grief has changed forever the person I am and will become as time goes on. I learn each day to become a new person, someone who survives, not in spite of the cruelty of others, but because of it. I have reached a point where I look over my shoulder at the old me, then turn ahead to move forward, proud of the journey I have embarked upon, and knowing that I have a long way to go.

I began to re-learn all of life, but with new eyes and a new heart, each tougher and more resilient. I guard against becoming callous or bitter. The new me laughs louder and more often, I speak with authority and boldness, standing tall instead of cowering in a dark place. I take paths that are new, untried and when I fall, I get back up and rejoice that I am *fearfully and wonderfully made.* I smile because I am a pearl of great price, a once-in-a-lifetime find and worth everything to possess.

I shake my head at the senselessness and cruelty of lying and cheating that murders the innocent as surely as a loaded gun. Adultery when perpetrated upon the trusting and innocent, the faithful and naïve, slays more than a marriage, it takes a life. It is said that you cannot un-ring the bell. Adulterers cannot un-do the charred remains of the hearts they have incinerated and laid upon the funeral pyre, all for their own selfish lust.

And today and every day I say with conviction, "I'm the best thing you'll ever have in your life, buddy."

Then I get up and dance.

EPILOGUE

My name is Danny; Daniel Joseph Pechacek. One in the same Danny depicted in this true life story, *Is It Too Late To Get My Money Back?*. Written by the love of my life, she has asked me if I would write the Epilogue.

After reading her book, I have come to some realizations about myself; some that are difficult to accept even after all these years and others of which I am very proud. I am in the autumn of my life; and life, as it always does, has made me wiser. I still have desires and wants, but those same desires and wants have grown to be in collaboration with my wife, Christine. As I read her book, I also realized what heartache I brought into her life. So many memories invade my heart and soul as I read her story, *our story*.

One memory is particularly stood out for me; the ectopic pregnancy. Christine lost our baby and nearly lost her life. I still vividly remember the dark sadness that came over me, realizing that I might lose my wife. I thanked God then for His grace in sparing her life. That day at the hospital, I asked God from my heart, my whole being, to please let Christine live. In that prayer, I told God that I would take her place, just let her live.

When I was a young teen, around fifteen years old, I was on my own as far as coming and going. I had a father and mother, and two younger sisters. I loved them all and I know I was loved in return. Life was good. At least I thought so. I had my own bedroom in our house, and plenty to eat. I felt like a top dog.

My parents always seemed to fight with each other. Our house seemed to be full of yelling and screaming on a daily basis. I know now that my parents were unfaithful to each other throughout their marriage. I am not in a position to judge their behavior. I was unfaithful to my lovely wife, Christine. My parents were so caught up in their own hell, they didn't have time to watch over me. I got away with things all the time. I could take off for a couple of days at a time and no one seemed to notice or care. I realize I got early training on how to manipulate and deceive young women. And I got very good at it. Damn good at it. I used that advantage nearly the rest of my life. And my wife suffered for it. We both ended up paying costly consequences.

Now, both of our lives have changed, for the better. Are there times we don't see eye-to-eye? Of course. But I realize that my wife is the kind of woman that refuses to settle for a husband, who won't stand up to, and for her and with her. Or better said, to have a set. After forty-seven years with this same woman, I *think* I understand her.

Yes, I do know this woman. We have had so many trials in our lives, as children, in our youth and as adults. Some we lost and many we have overcome, but no matter what, always together. Life can be and often is, unfair, but always invigorating. I believe it to be true that life is what you make of it and how you react to it.

I am proud of Christine as my wife, my lover, my friend, and a mother to our children. I am also proud of her ability to tackle tough jobs and to finish them, her writing and publishing. So when my wife, Christine, asked me to write an Epilogue, I was honored to do so.

And I told her so.

POSTSCRIPT

Four years ago on our way to the Florida Keys for the winter, Dan and I reminisced about growing up in Warren, Michigan. It was a way to pass the long hours of driving the same route for the third year. The highways and scenery never changed. You might think that having known each other since early childhood and being next-door neighbors, there would be little to share in the way of new revelations. The facts may not change, who we played with, the places we traversed, and the pastimes that occupied us as children, but age and distance have a way of giving new life to old memories. The pages in both of my books have opened windows into our lives, mine and Dan's. And not every vista is flattering.

I did not intend to put pen to paper as my own personal therapy but an amazing thing happened along the way. As I wrote spurts of memories, some funny, some sad and a few truly heart-breaking, my intention was to leave a history for my children and grand-children. Perhaps even my great-grandchildren. What astonished me was how liberating the process became as I remembered and wrote. It was as though putting the words on paper gave them a new life. The pages came alive. I found myself walking into the memories, looking on, and conversing with them. Watching the events unfold, I began to understand.

Writing the pages, telling my story has put to rest the rumblings held inside, out of sight, in a silent prison. For me, it was putting on new armor, heading straight into the battlefield and making my way to the front line of an ugly war that had gone on far too long. Walking in those mine-filled fields, and going head-to-head with my own demons made me realize that Christ has equipped me to be one tough soldier, fully equipped to do battle and win wars. Page after page, memory after memory, made more real to me His voice, His strength as I made the trek through some ugly places.

I did not write to expose dastardly deeds. It was never my intention that the pages should be an *Ah-ha!* Exposé. And certainly not a sword to slice and dice. This has first and foremost been a voyage into parts unknown to re-claim land stolen from not just me, but from both of us.

Our culture is a circus of sights and sounds, full of bright lights, loud music and dizzying aerial performances; all designed to keep our minds out of focus and wondering, fighting to just find balance. But like vertigo, eventually you are brought to your knees, unable to distinguish up from down, left from right, or light from dark. And tragically for some, right from wrong.

I lived that circus for four decades. All the glitter and sounds kept my attention and convinced me that my only reality was the life under the tent. My brief attempts to leave the circus ring resulted in those crazy clowns rushing out to hammer at me with their rubber mallets. And I immediately ran back under the tent to what I believed was safety. The glare and sights of the circus frightened me, made me unbalanced and even a little crazy, but I believed I had no choice. And so I accepted life under the big top as reality.

I love my children and grandchildren and I want them to see a life fully lived, a life of dark valleys and mountain tops, a life sometimes thrust into despair but always coming out victorious. That is what life *is*, the good and the not so good, joy and sorrow, feast and famine, but ultimately worth living to the fullest. We cannot allow *life* to dictate who we are or who we become. As cruel as it may seem at times, it is the flame of the furnace, the machinations of others that burn away the dross so we may become gold.

While the words penned are written from my own perspective, every page has been collaboration between Dan and me. I wrote. He read. We talked. We laughed and we cried.

In the movie *Parenthood*, Steve Martin and Mary Steenburgen, play a married couple coping with the sometimes utter chaos of everyday life. He feels overwhelmed. She tries to explain that, for her, life is a roller coaster ride; dizzying heights, sometimes sickening lows, and dangerous curves. One moment you are thrust upward to dangerous heights, and then just as dramatically, in a heartbeat, you fall and think you may not survive, but the ride is ultimately what makes it worth it all.

I agree.

Coming in 2014

Those Amazing Women

To learn more about Christine's upcoming events and for more information on *Tell Your Story, Leave Your Legacy©* go to: www.share-storymemories.com or christineauthor9@gmail.com

Made in the USA
Charleston, SC
23 May 2014